ROBUST RANGE IMAGE REGISTRATION

USING GENETIC ALGORITHMS AND THE SURFACE INTERPENETRATION MEASURE

SERIES IN MACHINE PERCEPTION AND ARTIFICIAL INTELLIGENCE*

Editors: **H. Bunke** (Univ. Bern, Switzerland)
P. S. P. Wang (Northeastern Univ., USA)

*For the complete list of titles in this series, please write to the Publisher.

Series in Machine Perception and Artificial Intelligence – Vol. 60

ROBUST RANGE IMAGE REGISTRATION

USING GENETIC ALGORITHMS AND THE SURFACE INTERPENETRATION MEASURE

Luciano Silva and Olga R P Bellon

Universidade Federal do Paraná, Brazil

Kim L Boyer

Ohio State University, USA

W **World Scientific**

NEW JERSEY • LONDON • SINGAPORE • BEIJING • SHANGHAI • HONG KONG • TAIPEI • CHENNAI

Published by

World Scientific Publishing Co. Pte. Ltd.

5 Toh Tuck Link, Singapore 596224

USA office: 27 Warren Street, Suite 401-402, Hackensack, NJ 07601

UK office: 57 Shelton Street, Covent Garden, London WC2H 9HE

British Library Cataloguing-in-Publication Data
A catalogue record for this book is available from the British Library.

ROBUST RANGE IMAGE REGISTRATION USING GENETIC ALGORITHMS AND THE SURFACE INTERPENETRATION MEASURE
Series in Machine Perception and Artificial Intelligence — Vol. 60

ISBN 981-256-108-0

Printed in Singapore by Mainland Press

Luciano Silva and Olga Bellon would like to dedicate this work to each other. Kim Boyer would like to dedicate this work to his family: wife Ann, son Jeff, and daughter Sandy.

Preface

The book addresses the range image registration problem for automatic 3D model construction. We focus on obtaining highly precise alignments between different view pairs of the same object to avoid 3D model distortions. In contrast to most prior work, the view pairs may exhibit relatively little overlap and need not be prealigned. To this end, we define a novel effective evaluation metric for registration, the Surface Interpenetration Measure (SIM). This measure quantifies the interleaving of two surfaces as their alignment is refined, putting the qualitative evaluation of "splotchiness", often used in reference to renderings of the aligned surfaces, onto a solid mathematical footing. The SIM is shown to be superior to mean squared error (i.e. more sensitive to fine scale changes) in controlling the final stages of the alignment process.

We then combine the SIM with Genetic Algorithms (GAs) to develop a robust approach for range image registration. The results confirm that this technique achieves precise surface registration with no need for prealignment, as opposed to methods based on the Iterative Closest Point (ICP) algorithm, the most popular to date. We present thorough experimental results, including an extensive comparative study and propose enhanced GA-based approaches to improve the registration still further. Additionally, we develop a global multiview registration technique using our GA-based approach. The results show considerable promise in terms of accuracy for 3D modeling.

L. Silva, Olga R.P. Bellon, Kim L. Boyer

Contents

Chapter 1

Introduction

Building realistic 3D models from sensor data is still a challenging problem. In recent years the demand for reconstruction and modeling of objects is increasing and it is widely used in many research areas, including medical imaging, robotic vision and archaeology [Ikeuchi and Sato (2001)]. Most applications focus on developing techniques to construct precise 3D object models of physical objects, preserving as much information as possible.

Recently, projects in digital archaeology have presented new challenges and are gaining popularity in computer vision community such as the Digital Michelangelo project [Levoy *et al.* (2000)] and the Great Buddha project [Ikeuchi and Sato (2001)]. A primary objective of these efforts is the digital preservation of cultural heritage objects before degradation or damage caused by environmental factors, erosion, fire, flood, or human development. Some collaborative efforts have supported the repair and restoration of historic buildings, construction of virtual museums, teaching using 3D visualization, and the analysis of complex structures by their 3D models [Bernardini *et al.* (2002)]. Additionally, in 2003 important conferences have organized sections to discuss the issue, such as the IEEE/CVPR Workshop on Applications of Computer Vision in Archaeology (ACVA'03) in association with the IEEE Conference on Computer Vision and Pattern Recognition and the Special Session on Heritage Applications of 4th International Conference on 3-D Digital Imaging and Modeling (3DIM'03).

Since a physical object cannot be completely scanned with a single image, multiple scans from different views are required to supply the information needed to construct the 3D model. The most important issues in this process are to minimize the number of views to reduce error accumulation in the 3D model and because data acquisition is expensive [Ikeuchi and Sato (2001)]. Therefore, it is fundamental to adopt a proper and robust technique to align the views in a common coordinate frame, *i.e.* a multiview registration process, to avoid model distortion in subsequent surface reconstruction stage.

There are many methods to perform the registration of views to create 3D models, including calibrated pose measurement and manual registration and verification [Turk and Levoy (1994), Ikeuchi and Sato (2001)]. By using mechanical equipment (*e.g.* robot arm or controlled turntable) to obtain the absolute poses for the scanner views, the calibrated pose methods generally are limited to small objects [Blais and Levine (1995)]. In manual registration and verification, time is the main problem because the user must search for corresponding feature points in the view pair by hand.

Typically, a 3D model is built by the alignment and integration of multiple range views (range images are described in Section 1.1) of an object or scene [Sharp *et al.* (2002), Dorai *et al.* (1998), Blais and Levine (1995), Huber and Hebert (2003), Reed and Allen (1999)]. These two basic steps can be performed sequentially or simultaneously. Usually, sequential methods [Turk and Levoy (1994), Chen and Medioni (1992)] result in imprecise object models since the transformations errors accumulate and propagate from one iteration to another. However, if one can guarantee precise transformations, this method is more attractive and requires less computation resources (*i.e* memory) than others.

The simultaneous method generally is a more robust way to reach precise 3D models. In this category, a global registration between all pairs of views is performed, followed by their integration [Ikeuchi and Sato (2001), Dorai *et al.* (1998), Shum *et al.* (1997), Masuda (2002)]. In this process the accumulation error between the previously registered views is distributed among all alignments, avoiding model distortions while preserving the geometry. Stoddart and Hilton [Stoddart and Hilton (1996)] proposed one of the first global registration methods based on a physical equivalent model. A similar approach was proposed by Eggert *et al.* [Eggert *et al.* (1998)] based on a multi-resolution framework. Bergevin *et al.* [Bergevin *et al.* (1996)] minimized the registration error of all views simultaneously using a well-balanced network of views. Huber and Hebert [Huber and Hebert (2003)] proposed a similar approach to find the minimum spanning tree in a graph, which represents possible model hypotheses for a set of views. Although these methods have been successfully applied in a number of cases, they have some drawbacks such as the computational complexity of the algorithms, and the loss of small details of the object because of imprecise alignments or error accumulation.

In the multiview registration process, the precise alignment of two views is the fundamental stage. Therefore, it is important to adopt a robust registration technique to properly avoid incorrect alignments and further model distortion. It is also important to minimize the number of views to be aligned and, consequently, the registration method must be able to deal with low-overlapped views. To reduce the complexity of the problem, most methods proposed for multiview registration perform an initial registration stage between each pair of overlapped views before the global registration process [Ikeuchi and Sato (2001)].

The registration process for two views consists of finding the best geometric transformation that, when applied to one view, aligns it with the other in a common coordinate system. When registering partially overlapped views, one of the most important issues is to develop methods to deal with low-overlapped views that can guarantee a precise alignment [Rodrigues *et al.* (2002)]. Recently, some papers have directly addressed the problem of calculating the overlapping area between views and measuring the registration quality [Huber and Hebert (2003), Silva *et al.* (2003e), Silva *et al.* (2003d), Dalley and Flynn (2002)]. In this book we show experiments using our robust registration method to align low-overlapped views. Our method is robust because it can deal with non-Gaussian noise, outliers and low-overlapped views.

Since the object's views are effectively aligned one can obtain the entire model by merging the views using a variety of well-known approaches for 3D model representation [Rusinliewicz and Levoy (2001b)]. Usually, a triangular mesh is used and further simplifications are performed to reduce the number of points in the model while preserving the shape of the object [Levoy *et al.* (2000)]. In addition, texture mapping of the reconstructed 3D surfaces is a challenging problem in creating realistic 3D models [Ikeuchi and Sato (2001)].

1.1 Range images

In recent years, range scanners have been improved, allowing an increased number of applications in important areas, such as digital archaeology [Bernardini *et al.* (2002)], building reconstruction and restoration [Reed and Allen (1999)], and medicine [Sinha *et al.* (2003)].

There is a number of range scanner models with distinct methods of acquisition and varying accuracy [Besl (1989)]. Some can acquire different images by combining time-of-flight (range image) and amplitude (reflectance image) of laser beams. These images can be combined to improve image processing stages, such as segmentation [Silva *et al.* (2002)] or edge-based representations [Silva *et al.* (2001)].

Most up-to-date range scanners use a laser beam to precisely measure the distance from the sensor to points in the surface of the object or scene [Besl (1989)], typically in a regular grid pattern as shown in Figure 1.1. This grid can be defined as a *range image* in which each pixel corresponds to a range sample. By defining the resolution of the range image one can obtain the 3D coordinates for each sampled point in the surface of the object. The range image is also known as a $2\frac{1}{2}D$ representation because the 3D information relates only to the visible surface of the object as seen from a given view point.

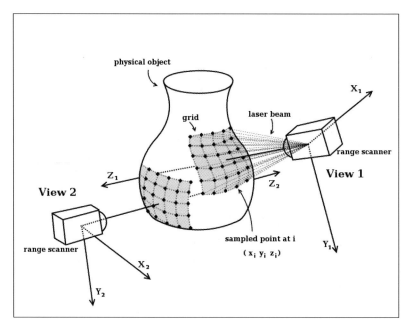

Fig. 1.1 Diagram of the range image acquisition process for two different views of the same object. The range images are composed by the sampled points of regular grids. Each sampled point has 3D information, (x_i, y_i, z_i), where i is a position on the grid.

More formally, a range image can be defined as a set of K discrete samples of a scalar function $j : \mathcal{I}^2 \rightarrow \mathcal{R}$, with $r_i = j(u_i)$, where $u_i \in \mathcal{I}^2$ is the index of the 2D grid (as shown in Figure 1.1), $r_i \in \mathcal{R}$ and $i = \{1, ..., K\}$.

A range image gives the distances between the image plane and points on the objects surfaces in the scene. By consulting a lookup table that indicates the relationship between the image coordinate system and the range scanner coordinate system, a range image can be further converted to range data. These are defined as a set of K discrete samples points of a vector function $h : \mathcal{I}^2 \rightarrow \mathcal{R}^3$, with $d_i = h(u_i)$, where $d_i \in \mathcal{R}^3$ and $i = \{1, ..., K\}$. Then, each sampled point has 3D coordinates (x_i, y_i, z_i).

Since that only part of the object can be seen from any given view point, multiple views are needed to obtain the entire 3D surface of a physical object (see Figure 1.1). Also, it is necessary that these views have some overlap to allow their registration. As can be seen in Figure 1.1 there is no overlap between views 1 and 2. Figure 1.2 shows an example of a range image in which it is possible to note unseen regions on the object surface when it is observed from differents points of view.

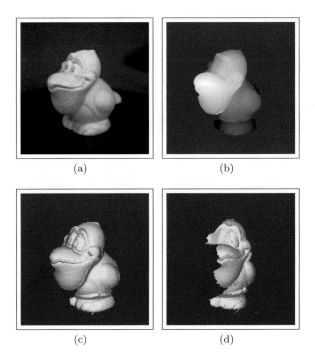

(a)   (b)

(c)   (d)

Fig. 1.2 An example of range image acquired with the Minolta Vivid 700 scanner: (a) the picture of the object; (b) the range image, in which the lighter pixels are closer to the sensor than the dark ones; (c) and (d) two rendered views of the range image of (a) observed from different points of view.

In this book we work with several different range image databases, some are available on the Internet and others were kindly supplied by research groups, as listed bellow:

- OSU range image database: Maintained by the Signal Analysis and Machine Perception Laboratory (SAMPL) at The Ohio State University - USA, coordinated by Prof. Kim L. Boyer. We used the range images from different small objects acquired with the Minolta Vivid 700 range scanner. Each object was imaged in 18 views acquired at 20 degree intervals using a computer-controlled turntable (`http://sampl.eng.ohio-state.edu`).

- IMAGO range image database: Maintained by the IMAGO group at the Universidade Federal do Paran - Brazil, coordinated by Prof. Olga R.P. Bellon. The images of small objects with high resolution and precision were acquired using the Roland MDX-15 scanner (`http://www.inf.ufpr.br/imago`).

- The Digital Michelangelo Project: Developed at Stanford University - USA, coordinated by Prof. Marc Levoy. This database has a number of range images from many statues created by Michelangelo in Italy. The images were acquired with high resolution using a special scanner fabricated for them by Cyberware (`http://graphics.stanford.edu/projects/mich`).

- The Great Temple in Petra: Supplied by Prof. Frederic Leymarie of the SHAPE lab at Brown University - USA. The images were acquired with a ShapeGrabber laser scanner in June 2002 at the site of the Great Temple in Petra, Jordan (`http://www.lems.brown.edu/vision/extra/SHAPE`).

- The Cathedral of Saint Pierre: Supplied by Prof. Peter Allen of the Robotics Group at Columbia University - USA. The images were acquired with a Cyrax 2400 scanner in 2001 for a project to model the Cathedral of Saint Pierre, Beauvais, France (`http://www1.cs.columbia.edu/~allen/BEAUVAIS`).

- The Thomas Hunter Building: Supplied by Prof. Ioannis Stamos of Hunter College - USA. The external views of the Thomas Hunter building in New York were acquired with a Cyrax 2400 scanner.

- Stuttgart range image database: This database contains a collection of synthetic range images with different view points taken from high-resolution polygonal models available on the web (`http://range.informatik.uni-stuttgart.de`).

We performed several experiments using these databases to compare our methods for range image registration with others and the results are reported in this book. Additionally, we performed some exhaustive evaluations using the OSU range image database to prove statistically the efficiency of our methods, as presented in the following chapters.

1.2 Applications

There are many applications for which it is desirable to generate 3D models of real objects, including object recognition, robot navigation and reverse engineering [Brown (1992)]. However, most do not demand a precise 3D model to achieve their objective.

In some applications, such as digital archaeology, it is essential to obtain precise 3D models since the objective is to preserve historic sites with as much information and detail as possible [Ikeuchi and Sato (2001)]. In this context, it is important to develop a robust range image registration method that is able to precisely align views of the object, generally by using a set of range images. In this book we address this problem and develop a robust method expected to be useful for many applications, including:

- Archaeology - Creating digital replicas of huge sculptures for heritage preservation. Thus, archaeologists can share their sites for in-depth investigation by other research groups. We can list some important contribution in this area, such as the Digital Michelangelo project [Levoy *et al.* (2000)], the Great Buddha project [Ikeuchi and Sato (2001)] and the Piet project [Bernardini *et al.* (2002)].
- Museology - Generating reproductions of memorable statues and sculptures from different places around the world to make them available in other museums. Furthermore, one can provide virtual visits to virtual museums to visualize the 3D models remotely.
- Architecture - Providing realistic environments from a set of views of buildings for structural analysis. Precise 3D models can aid building construction by providing information regarding different stages for visual inspection or automatic measurements. Also, for building reconstruction or restoration, it is important to plan and to test the proposed project in advance using 3D models to reduce potential the damage to historical sites.
- Military - Providing a robust registration method to deal with clut-

tered environments for many applications, such as target detection and object recognition, in which precision is a fundamental concern.

- Medicine - For critical processes, such as neurosurgery, the 3D models need to be reliable to avoid irreversible damage [Sinha *et al.* (2003)]. Additionally, the practice of dentistry requires accurate 3D representations for the study of the evolution of clinical treatments [Ahmed *et al.* (1997)].

1.3   Book outline

The remainder of this book is organized as follows: Chapter 1.3 presents the background of range image registration with related work and provides the strengths and weaknesses of each approach. Chapter 2.5 introduces a novel evaluation measure, called the Surface Interpenetration Measure (SIM), to assess the quality of registration results and to guide the registration process. We also present a number of experiments to show the stability of this measure. Chapter 3.5 presents the main concepts of Genetic Algorithms as applied to range image registration and shows experiments performed with different strategies. Chapter 4.10 describes a robust range image registration combining Genetic Algorithms (GAs) and the SIM. We also provide an in-depth discussion of the experiments with several comparison results. In Chapter 5.4 we describe experiments in multiview range image registration using our GA-based method with a critical analysis comparing it with other related approaches. Finally, in Chapter 6.5 we conclude by summarizing the contributions of this book and discussing directions for future work.

Chapter 2

Range Image Registration

This chapter investigates different approaches for the range image registration problem and discusses their strengths and weaknesses. We also introduce the problem of obtaining precise alignments and how to identify and quantify them. We begin by formally defining the range image registration problem in Section 2.1. Next, in Section 2.2 we describe and discuss distinct approaches for range image registration. Section 2.3 presents the main outlier rejection rules used to avoid erroneous correspondences between point pairs in the registration process. Finally, in Section 2.4 we present the registration quality measures generally used to evaluate the registration results. In Section 2.5 we summarize the main ideas and the content of this chapter.

2.1 Definition

The goal of the registration task is to find the transformation that best represents the relative displacement between two surfaces having a common overlapping area. In fact, how to efficiently estimate this transformation is one of the main issues in registration [Rodrigues *et al.* (2002)].

For the registration of two range images, A and B, the goal is to estimate the 3D rigid motion, represented by the transformation T, that best aligns the points in A with the points in B [Horn (1986)]. We can define T by a 3×3 rotation matrix R and a 3D translation vector t, with $T = (R, t)$. A rigid motion of a 3D point p is given by a linear transformation as $T(p) = Rp + t$. The transformation applied to a set of n points $P = \{p_i\}$ with $i = \{1, ..., n\}$ is represented by $T(P) = \{Rp_i + t\}$.

We can parameterize T with a vector $\nu = [\theta_x, \theta_y, \theta_z, t_x, t_y, t_z]$, where θ_x, θ_y and θ_z are rotation angles about the x, y and z axes (the X-Y-

Z Euler angles) and t_x, t_y and t_z are the components of the translation vector [Horn (1986)].

2.2   Registration approaches

The main differences among range image registration methods are the techniques to find corresponding points between views and to estimate the transformation to align the views. Also, some methods make use of image features other than points, such as edge maps and surface curvatures, to guide the registration process [Sappa *et al.* (2001)].

Clearly, if there is no overlap between the views, it is impossible to align them by only analyzing their 3D points (see Figure 1.1, page 4). Therefore, it is necessary to provide a significant overlapping area between views in the acquisition process to allow them to be registered. In this book we address this issue.

Several registration approaches have been proposed during the last decade. They can be classified basically into two distinct groups: *coarse registration* and *fine registration* techniques. In coarse registration the goal is to find a set of approximate registration transformations without prior knowledge of the relative spatial positions of the views. Most of these methods are based on finding correspondences between distinctive features that may be present in the overlapping area. The basic procedure involves the identification of features, assignment of feature correspondences, and alignment based on these correspondences. There are many different features that can be explored: edge maps [Sappa *et al.* (2001)], lines and planes [Faugeras and Hebert (1986)], bitangent curves [Wyngaerd and Gool (2002)], surface curvatures [Yamany and Farag (1999), Chua and Jarvis (1996)], surface orientation [Johnson and Hebert (1999)] and invariant features, such as moments and curvature [Sharp *et al.* (2002)].

Sappa *et al.* [Sappa *et al.* (2001)] presented a method using an edge-based segmentation technique to guide the registration process. Chua and Jarvis [Chua and Jarvis (1996)] used principal curvatures and Darboux frames to compute invariant features. Also, Feldmar and Ayache [Feldmar and Ayache (1996)] proposed a method to estimate rigid displacements by using principal curvatures of surfaces.

Stein and Medioni [Stein and Medioni (1992)] proposed the splash structure, which is a local map describing the distribution of surface normals along a geodesic circle. The *spin image* presented by Johnson and

Hebert [Johnson and Hebert (1999)], which is a data level shape descriptor, have been used in registration [Huber and Hebert (2003)]. Lucchese *et al.* [Lucchese *et al.* (2002)] exploit the geometric regularity obtained by the Fourier transform as a frequency domain-based method for range image registration. The RANSAC-based DARCES of Chen*et al.* [Chen *et al.* (1999)] is a robust method based on exhaustive search that can check all possible data alignments between two given sets of points to register two partially overlapped views.

Because of the difficulty in calculating precise transformations, the coarse registration methods generally supply only rough alignments. In contrast, fine registration approaches are based on the assumption that a good initial transformation (*i.e.* close to the solution) was previously obtained. Then, precise alignments may be obtained with reliable criteria to measure the quality of the refined transformations. Additionally, a number of registration approaches in the literature proposed to combine both techniques, a coarse registration followed by a fine registration, to achieve automatic and precise registration results [Huber and Hebert (2003)], [Sappa *et al.* (2001), Chen *et al.* (1999)].

The best-known methods for fine range image registration are variations on the Iterative Closest Point (ICP) algorithm [Besl and McKay (1992)]. ICP is an iterative procedure minimizing the mean squared error (MSE), computed by the sum of the squared distances between points in one view and the closest points, respectively, in the other view. In each ICP iteration, the best geometric transformation that aligns the two images is calculated.

The ICP algorithm is composed of two basic procedures: one to find correspondences between points and another to estimate the transformations iteratively from the point correspondences until some termination criteria are satisfied. As reported by Besl and McKay [Besl and McKay (1992)], the correspondence search consumes about 95% of the runtime. Then, given two range images $A = \{a_i\}$ and $B = \{b_j\}$ with $i = \{1, ..., n\}$ and $j = \{1, ..., m\}$ the goal of the iterative process of the algorithm is to minimize the following function:

$$f(R,t) = \frac{1}{n}\sum_{i=1}^{n}||a_i - Rb_j - t||^2 \qquad (2.1)$$

where b_j is the closest point in B to the point $a_i \in A$, R the rotation matrix and t the translation vector.

To find R and t one can use singular value decomposition or orthonormal matrices [Arun *et al.* (1987), Horn *et al.* (1988)]. The correspondence between points is usually performed by a nearest-neighbor search using k-d tree structure for optimization [Bentley (1975)]. The k-d tree is a spatial data structure originally proposed to allow efficient search on orthogonal range queries and nearest neighbor queries [Bentley (1975)]. Recently, Greenspan and Godin [Greenspan and Godin (2001)] proposed a significant improvement in the nearest neighbor queries by using correspondences of previous iterations of the ICP and searching only in their small neighborhood to update the correspondences. Another important strategy to speed up the registration process uses sampling techniques to reduce the number of points in the views [Rusinliewicz and Levoy (2001a)].

Nevertheless, the proper convergence of ICP is guaranteed only if one of the datasets is a subset of the other; otherwise, erroneous alignments can result. Although ICP is efficient, with average case complexity of $O(n \log n)$ for n point images, it converges monotonically to a local minimum.

Another drawback of ICP is that it requires a good pre-alignment of the views to converge to a correct solution. Many variants of the ICP have been proposed [Levoy *et al.* (2000), Sharp *et al.* (2002), Chen and Medioni (1992), Rusinliewicz and Levoy (2001a), Liu and Rodrigues (2002)] to overcome these limitations. For registration with partial overlap, heuristics have been proposed to ignore non-overlapped regions [Rusinliewicz and Levoy (2001a)] and consequently to obtain more effective transformations. Section 2.3 addresses these methods. Figure 2.1 shows two registration results by an ICP-based method [Levoy *et al.* (2000)] using the same pair of range views, but in one a pre-alignment was applied before the registration procedure. As can be seen, without pre-alignment ICP converged to a completely erroneous result.

The main differences among these various proposals are in the evaluation functions to measure the quality of the alignments in each iteration and outlier rejection rules, such as discarding boundary points since they are more likely to yield false matches [Levoy *et al.* (2000)]. Chen and Medioni [Chen and Medioni (1992)] developed an approach which minimizes the sum of squared distance between points in one view to a local tangent plane in the other view. Correspondences are formed by projecting the points onto the other view in the direction of their normal vectors (point-to-plane search) rather than searching for their closest point (point-to-point search). This approach is relatively faster than traditional ICP and usually the final results are better if a good initial pre-alignment is provided. However, this approach presents some numerical and search limitations since

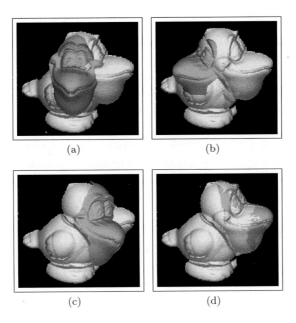

Fig. 2.1 Registration results by ICP for a pair of range images: (a) initial views positions without any pre-alignment; (b) the registration result starting from the views positioned as in (a); (c) pre-aligned views; and (d) the registration result from views positioned as in (c).

some correspondences may not be found [Chen and Medioni (1992)].

Zhang [Zhang (1994)] proposed a sophisticated set of modifications to ICP and his method has been used in many recent registration systems. The method automatically computes a threshold that is used to classify a point as an outlier if its distance from the corresponding point exceeds this threshold. By removing outliers from the registration calculations, one can estimate more precise transformations.

Masuda and Yokoya [Masuda and Yokoya (1995)] proposed a robust method for registering a pair of dense range images, that integrates ICP, random sampling, and the least median squares estimator (LMS). They also proposed a modification of the k-d tree structure to improve the search and speed up the method.

A careful analysis of these various approaches reveals their true strengths and weaknesses [Liu and Rodrigues (2002)]. In addition, comparative studies of variants of the ICP have been done [Dalley and Flynn (2002), Rusinliewicz and Levoy (2001a)], but it is difficult to evaluate these comparisons because there is neither a common image database, nor well defined metrics. Recently, a special issue on the registration and fusion of range images [Rodrigues *et al.* (2002)] presents a great overview of different registration approaches.

The common lesson in these comparative studies is that, while ICP continues to undergo development and extension, progress on this front has become asymptotic; further improvements are likely to be incremental, at best. The characteristics of ICP that limit its effectiveness in domains where robustness is required and pre-alignment is infeasible remain. Occasionally, the strategies to overcome the pre-alignment limitation may guide the convergence process to an erroneous solution. What is needed is a fundamentally different search approach, including a robust assessment of alignment quality.

Another promising approach to register two range images is to find the geometric transformation through a pose-space search [Robertson and Fisher (2002)], rather than the correspondence-based search of ICP-based methods. In this case, the goal is to find, in a huge search space of geometric transformations, a solution that can be used to align precisely two views, in a reasonable time. One way to perform this search is through efficient stochastic optimization techniques, such as Genetic Algorithms (GAs) [Man *et al.* (1996)] and Simulated Annealing (SA) [Kirkpatrick *et al.* (1983)]. This approach is generally considered to provide coarse registration. However, one can combine different operators, such as local search heuristics, to obtain precise alignments during the convergence process. In that way, the final registration results can be compared with traditional fine registration approaches.

In this book we perform an extensive study using enhanced GA approaches for range image registration. We focus on the problem of obtaining precise alignments of range views through a robust registration method using views that are only partially overlapped. To support this, we define and use a new robust measure, the Surface Interpenetration Measure (SIM), to calculate the interpenetration of two registered range views, presented in Chapter 2.5.

2.3   Outlier rejection rules

The iterative search for corresponding points, as in ICP-based approaches, has become the dominant method for aligning range images because of its simplicity and efficiency. Given their main limitations, such as pre-alignment and local convergence, comparisons between different methods suggest a combination of heuristics to obtain a more robust ICP variant [Rusinliewicz and Levoy (2001a)]. Most of these heuristics are related to outlier rejection rules to discard erroneous corresponding points.

In aligning partially overlapped range images, the points in regions without any correspondence must be labeled as outliers to avoid imprecise estimation of the transformation and consequently to prevent erroneous registration results [Levoy *et al.* (2000)].

One of the most effective outlier rejection rules is to exclude corresponding pairs that include points on the boundaries of the images [Levoy *et al.* (2000)]. This rule is especially useful for avoiding erroneous pairings because in 3D modeling from range images the overlap between views is incomplete. The computational cost to apply this rule is usually low and has few drawbacks. Figure 2.2 offers a diagram to illustrate this rule where we see that the correspondences including points on boundaries can introduce a systematic bias into the alignment.

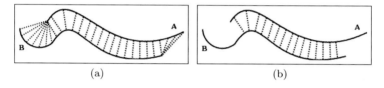

(a) (b)

Fig. 2.2 Example of corresponding points between two range views *A* and *B*: (a) with no outlier rejection rule and (b) after eliminating corresponding points on the boundaries.

Another traditional rule applied in most registration approaches is to use a threshold to eliminate pairs with larger corresponding distance. In [Schutz *et al.* (1998)] the authors defined the threshold empirically based on the separation of the centers of mass of the images. Zhang [Zhang (1994)] computes the threshold dynamically for each iteration based on the mean point pair distance and the standard deviation of the distances. Masuda and Yokoya [Masuda and Yokoya (1995)] defines the threshold empirically to be 2.5σ, where σ signifies the standard deviation of residuals estimated by a robust estimator based on least median of squares. Also, in [Levoy *et al.* (2000)] the threshold is defined as a percentage of pairs with the largest corresponding distances. The main problem in defining the rule is how to set the threshold to deal with different range images and to guarantee precise alignments. In fact, this important issue has been explored elsewhere in computer vision and image processing research [Haddon (1988), Sahoo *et al.* (1988)].

Recently, Huber and Hebert [Huber and Hebert (2003)] explored a combination of outlier rejection rules to define the overlapping region between views. They define a set of constraints to discard erroneous corresponding pairs, such as maximum distance between pairs and the maximum angle between the normal vectors of the pair. They also used the rule of eliminating points on the boundaries.

Generally, the rejection of outliers does not help with initial convergence, but it may improve the accuracy and stability with which the correct alignment is determined [Rusinliewicz and Levoy (2001a)]. Usually, because of the difficulty of threshold selection the resulting registration may present local misalignment. Additionally, we have observed that even with a low threshold a precise alignment may not be guaranteed (see Chapter 2.5). We report some tests using these related outlier rejection rules in Chapter 2.5 and successfully apply them to our registration approach, in Chapter 4.10.

2.4   Registration quality measures

One of the main difficulties in evaluating registration results is acquiring the "ground truth" registration of two views. Some papers present quantitative evaluation metrics applying randomly chosen transformations to one view from a pair of aligned views (usually obtained from synthetic range data), and performing the registration [Rusinliewicz and Levoy (2001a)]. After registration a mean distance is computed between the points of the transformed view before the transformations and after the registration, since the true corresponding points are known.

In registering real range images the true point correspondences are difficult   to   obtain   even   through   calibrated   ranging systems [Blais and Levine (1995)]. Therefore, erroneous alignments can generate a small inter-point error, giving a misleading (optimistic) measure because of the incorrect estimation of corresponding points. This error is usually computed by the mean squared error (MSE) between corresponding points of two images after the registration process.

Another problem is to define the minimum overlapping area between two views needed to guarantee a precise alignment. If there exists inadequate overlap between the views the registration process may generate erroneous solutions. In fact, to address this problem it is necessary to evaluate the registration method used before undertaking an exhaustive acquisition of multiple views [Ikeuchi and Sato (2001)].

A similar situation occurs in multiview registration in identifying over-lapped views to be registered to generate a full 3D model. Huber and Hebert proposed a "brute force" method [Huber and Hebert (2003)] per-forming exhaustive registrations between each pair of views and searching for a network of views with the lowest global error. They define a set of evaluation metrics to identify incorrect alignments based on the visibility of the registration and overlapping areas. By analyzing the z-buffer of the registration scene and the direction of the scanning process they can iden-tify if there are occluding areas of a view and in this case the alignment is identified as an erroneous registration result.

Also, they define the concept of overlapped points in two range images based on three conditions: 1) the closest point distance between the point in one view and its corresponding point in the other view is less than a threshold t_1; 2) the points cannot be on the boundary of either image; and 3) the angle between the surface normal at the point in one view and the surface normal at its corresponding point in the other view is less than a threshold t_2. In their implementation, t_1 is estimated from the mean dis-tance residuals at each iteration and t_2 is set at 45 degrees. The problem in using t_1 is that for imprecise alignment some parallel regions have a very low inter-point error and may be incorrectly labeled as overlapped regions. Also, threshold t_2 and condition 2 can only eliminate a small fraction of points. Consequently, the most important condition, and the main draw-back, is to define a reasonable t_1. Usually, only clearly outlying points are eliminated with this criterion; it cannot define overlapping regions pre-cisely. We performed some comparisons by using this strategy to evaluate registrations, as presented in Chapter 2.5.

Visual comparisons can provide qualitative evaluation of registration us-ing real range images. Dalley and Flynn [Dalley and Flynn (2001)] suggest that a good registration must present a large "splotchy" surface, which is the visual result of two surfaces, each rendered in a different color, cross-ing over each other repeatedly in the overlapping area. This effect can be described as the *interpenetration* of the two surfaces. However, it is impos-sible to measure the degree of interpenetration by visual inspection alone because the resulting image depends on a variety of factors, such as render-ing resolution, illumination, image sampling, surface representation, etc. At best we gain a qualitative assessment. Moreover, as a qualitative as-sessment, "splotchiness" provides no useful control mechanism to guide the registration process. Figure 2.3 shows two registrations obtained with ICP using range images, presented in [Dalley and Flynn (2001)], to illustrate the "splotchiness" effect.

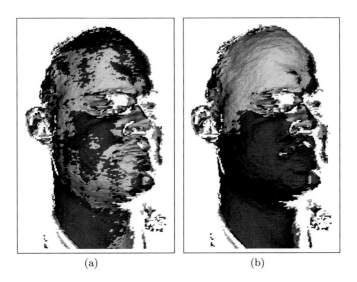

(a)   (b)

Fig. 2.3 Examples of registration to illustrate the "splotchiness" effect (from [Dalley and Flynn (2001)]): (a) good "splotchiness" and (b) poor "splotchiness".

We investigated the definition of a new measure based on the quantification of *interpenetration* effect that may represent a potential measure to identify precise alignments. Chapter 2.5 discusses in detail our experiments based on this measure.

2.5   Summary

This chapter has presented the concepts of range image registration and related work. We considered different approaches to the registration problem and highlighted their main advantages and drawbacks. We observed that one of the main issues in range image registration for partially overlapped views are the outlier rejection rules to avoid erroneous corresponding points and evaluation measures to quantify the obtained alignments.

Chapter 3

Surface Interpenetration Measure (SIM)

This chapter describes a novel evaluation metric, which we call the Surface Interpenetration Measure (SIM), to calculate the overlapping area between views and precisely measure the quality of the alignments from range image registration. First, we present the definition of the SIM in Section 3.1. Section 3.2 discusses how to obtain precise alignments using the SIM. In Section 3.3 we show the results of the SIM for different parameters and constraints. Experimental results to show the stability of the SIM against noise are presented in Section 3.4. We conclude this chapter with a discussion of the results obtained by this new measure in Section 3.5.

3.1 Definition

We define the surface interpenetration by analyzing different visual results of two aligned surfaces, each rendered in a different color, crossing over each other repeatedly in the overlapping area. The interpenetration effect results from the nature of real range data, which presents slightly rough surfaces with small local distortions caused by limitations in the precision of the acquiring sensor or by noise. Because of this, even flat surfaces (*e.g.* polished plate made of wood or metal) present a "roughness" in range images, as can be seen in Figure 3.1. We also observed that two views acquired from the same object surface with the same scanner position and parameters provide two different range images.

By performing the registration of two range images of flat surfaces, we can confirm that there are interpenetrating regions between them. With this, we can assume that independently of the surfaces' shapes the interpenetration will always occur. Figure 3.2 shows the interpenetration effect between the two range images, shown in Figures 3.1(a) and 3.1(b). In Fig-

19

ure 3.3 a set of parallel scan lines were extracted from the range image shown in Figures 3.1(a), to better illustrate the "roughness" of the surface. These scan lines are cross sections of the surface, all obtained in the same direction.

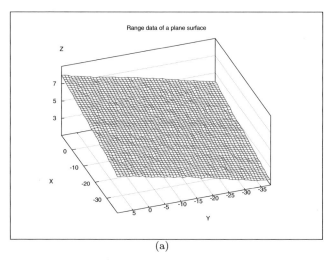

(a)

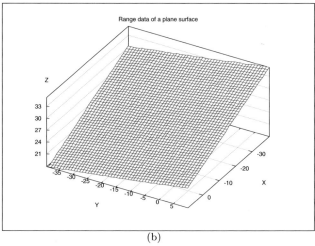

(b)

Fig. 3.1   Plots of two range images (a) and (b), acquired from different views of a planar surface (a polished plate made of metal). As can be seen, the images present a slightly rough surface caused by limitations of precision in the range sensor. These range datasets were obtained by researchers of the SAMPL at OSU, using a Minolta Vivid 700 laser scanner.

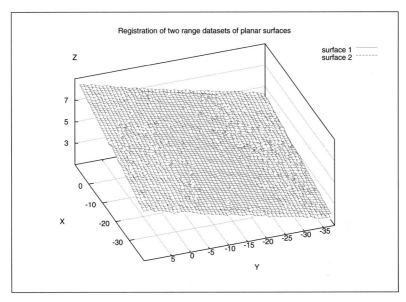

Fig. 3.2 Plots of the two registered range data of Figure 3.1 to verify the interpenetration effect after registration of plane surfaces (please view in color for best effect).

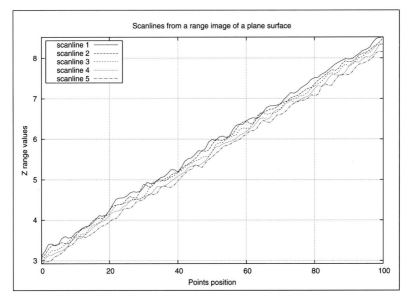

Fig. 3.3 Plots of parallel scan lines (cross sections) in the range image shown in Figure 3.1(a) to illustrate the "roughness" of a planar surface.

By quantifying interpenetration, we can more precisely evaluate registration results and provide a highly robust control. To do this we developed the following measure based on the surface normal vector, computed by a local least squares planar fit [Pratt (1987)], at each point. After the alignment of two images, A and B, we identify the set of interpenetrating points in A with respect to B. For each point $p \in A$ we define a neighborhood N_p to be a small $n \times n$ window centered on p. We choose $n = 5$ based on the observation that the interpenetration is a local effect, as will be presented in the experiments of Section 3.3.

With q denoting a point in the neighborhood N_p, c the corresponding point of p in image B (computed by a point-to-point nearest neighbor search using a k-d tree structure for optimization [Bentley (1975)]) and $\vec{n}_c$ the local surface normal at c, we define the set of interpenetrating points as:

$$C_{(A,B)} = \{p \in A \mid [(\overrightarrow{q_i - c}) \cdot \vec{n}_c][(\overrightarrow{q_j - c}) \cdot \vec{n}_c] < 0\} \qquad (3.1)$$

where $q_i, q_j \in N_p$ and $i \neq j$. This set comprises those points in A whose neighborhoods include at least one pair of points separated by the local tangent plane, computed at their correspondents in B, as can be seen in the diagram of Figure 3.4.

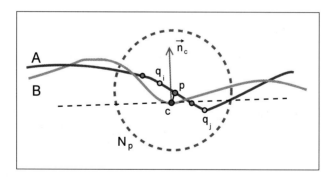

Fig. 3.4   Interpenetrating point p in A with respect to B.

With this, we then define the Surface Interpenetration Measure as the fraction of interpenetrating points in A:

$$SIM_{(A,B)} = \frac{|C_{(A,B)}|}{|A|} \qquad (3.2)$$

We also performed experiments using a point-to-plane search approach [Chen and Medioni (1992)] in Eq. 3.1, and the results are quite similar for precise alignments, but with some numerical limitations for erroneous alignments. A registration of two surfaces that presents a good interpenetration has a high SIM value. We also can analyze the distribution of the interpenetrating points by generating a binary image from the SIM calculation. Figure 3.5 offers an example of different alignments of two views with 100% of overlap. In this example both images are of the same view, but small rigid transformations were applied to one of them to simulate a misalignment in the registration process. After that, for each point the normal vectors are computed and the search for corresponding points was performed to give the necessary inputs for the SIM calculation (see Eq. 3.1).

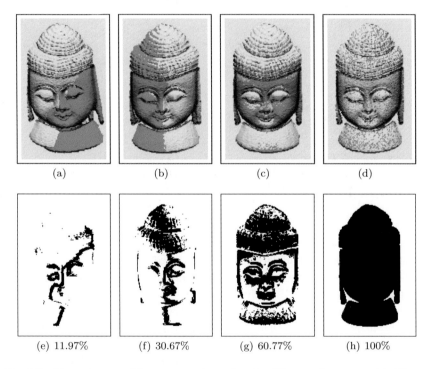

(a)	(b)	(c)	(d)
(e) 11.97%	(f) 30.67%	(g) 60.77%	(h) 100%

Fig. 3.5 Binary images of interpenetrating points for different alignments: (a)-(d) are simulated alignments to compute the SIM and (e)-(h) are their binary images and SIM values obtained from the Eq. 3.2, respectively. The alignment shown in (d) was obtained with no transformation, *i.e.* both images A and B are the same range image.

Our experimental results show that erroneous alignments produce low SIM values and that *small differences in MSE can yield significant differ-*

ences in SIM. Furthermore, alignments with high SIM present a very low interpoint-error between surfaces. That is, the interpenetration measure is a far more sensitive indicator of alignment quality when comparing "reasonable" alignments. Also, the SIM is simple to compute and have linear time complexity $O(n)$ independently on the number of points in the image.

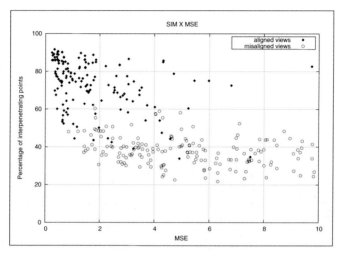

Fig. 3.6   Results for 496 alignments obtained by exhaustive ICP-based registration. The classifications are based on visual analysis totaling: 166 "aligned" views and 330 "misaligned" views. The units of MSE are in terms of range values.

Figure 3.6 demonstrates the results of the MSE and SIM measures for different alignments. In this experiment we computed 496 alignments obtained by exhaustive ICP-based registrations using point-to-point and point-to-plane correspondence methods [Besl and McKay (1992), Chen and Medioni (1992)]. Different combinations of adjacent views of four objects were used, totaling 124 alignments for each object. Each object has 18 views acquired using a turntable with 20 degrees between adjacent views and we combined views separated by 20 and 40 degrees (see Appendix 7.2, page 125 for details of the objects and registration results obtained in this experiment). Then, we classified each obtained registration as "aligned" or "misaligned" by visual inspection and computed the MSE and SIM. Although the subjective aspect of this experiment in evaluating registration results, we can observe the general trends of the measures. The 166 "aligned" views presented a good matching between surfaces of the views while preserving details of the objects. For example, the registrations obtained in Figure 2.3 must be considered "aligned". The 330 "misaligned" views are those in which mismatched regions between surfaces are identified and consequently did not preserve details of the objects.

As can be seen in the plot (see Figure 3.6) it is difficult to distinguish correct from incorrect alignments using only the MSE, since "misaligned" and "aligned" views may present similar MSE values. In contrast, one can easily use the SIM to identify more precisely correct alignments, for instance views with more than 60% in the SIM. We observe in this plot that some correct alignments exhibit high MSE because we applied no constraint in the MSE calculation, such as outlier rejection. We provide the same plot using different constraints in the SIM calculation, in Section 3.3, to show improvements and the stability of this new measure.

Intuitively, it is possible to assess the quality the registration using both MSE and SIM, without a visual verification. Of course, the SIM measure alone is not enough to determine if an alignment is correct, but it can confirm a good result when analyzed together with the resulting MSE [Silva *et al.* (2003e), Silva *et al.* (2003c)]. We present the results of combining both measures in Chapter 4.10.

We performed several experiments to explore performance of SIM with respect to different parameters and constraints applied to Eq. 3.1. These experiments are presented in the following sections.

3.2 Obtaining precise alignments

We performed a number of experiments to evaluate the registration results in terms of SIM and MSE. The idea was to confirm that the SIM is a robust sensitive indicator of alignment quality for different alignments using partially overlapped views. One of the main advantages of the SIM is that one can identify precise registrations for good alignments. For instance, a correct alignment with low MSE may have no interpenetration if the aligned surfaces are parallel. However, by using the SIM we can reach a precise alignment with a high SIM while preserving a low MSE. Besides, many authors have reported that there may exist several local solutions for good alignments when the evaluation of registrations are computed by MSE [Sharp *et al.* (2002), Huber and Hebert (2003)]. Figure 3.7 shows some situations where MSE may fail in evaluating precise registrations.

To evaluate and compare SIM *vs.* MSE measures, we performed a number of registrations using different combinations of aligned views with unequal overlapping areas (see Chapter 3.5 for a discussion of the minimum overlap required to provide precise alignments using our methods). The alignments between views were obtained using: (1) a variant of the ICP [Levoy *et al.* (2000)], used to obtain precise alignments in the Michelangelo project, and (2) our robust approach to range image registration using Genetic Algorithms, as presented in Chapter 4.10. In these experiments, for some views it was necessary to perform a manual pre-alignment to obtain a correct registration by the ICP approach.

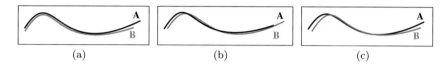

Fig. 3.7   Different alignments of two range images A and B with low MSE: (a) parallel surfaces; (b) surfaces that cross each other over different regions and (c) misaligned surfaces presenting regions with very low MSE.

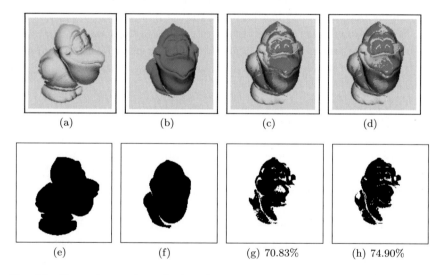

Fig. 3.8   Binary images from the SIM for the alignment between views (a) and (b). Figures (e) and (f) are the respective binary images of (a) and (b), which represent points on the surface of the object; (c) and (d) show the alignment obtained by ICP and by our GA-based method (see Chapter 4.10), respectively; (g) and (h) show the SIM of the alignments in (c) and (d), respectively with (f) serving as A in the SIM calculation.

Figure 3.8 shows an example from the experiments of two-view registration, in which the view of Figure 3.8(a) has approximately 55% overlapping points in the view of Figure 3.8(b), and Figure 3.8(b) has approximately 75% overlapping points in the view of Figure 3.8(a). These overlap measurements were defined based on the best SIM values obtained for this view pair. The results of MSE and SIM for Figure 3.8 are: (c) MSE= 6.8701 and SIM= 70.83%; (d) MSE= 6.8887 and SIM= 74.90%. In this example the MSE was computed for all corresponding points between views without constraints.

We observed that the results of Figures 3.8(c) and 3.8(d) show correct alignments and similar MSE values. Although the MSE of the ICP result is lower, the SIM shows that the alignment of Figure 3.8(d) has approximately 4% more interpenetrating points than that of Figure 3.8(c). This represents more than 250 of the 6309 points of the surface of the object of Figure 3.8(b).

By analyzing local areas in the surfaces of different correct alignments we see that the SIM better distributes the registration error over the entire alignment. Because ICP-based approaches are guided by the MSE, the results present generally a low global registration error, but the distribution of this error is not uniform, as can be confirmed in the histograms of Figure 3.9 and Figure 3.10. These histograms were obtained using the correct alignments of Figure 3.8. Figure 3.9(a) presents a greater fraction of corresponding points with low MSE than does Figure 3.9(b).

If we analyze the number of interpenetrating points and their corresponding point distances within a very low distance range, we see that our approach has a higher fraction of interpenetrating points compared to the ICP results. Because of this, the blue lines (interpenetrating points) in Figure 3.10(b) are closer to the black lines (all points) than in Figure 3.10(a) with the same analysis. Also, the number of non-interpenetrating points (red lines) in Figure 3.10(a), even with very low distances, is higher in Figure 3.10(a) because in some regions of the alignment the surfaces are parallel.

We investigated the interpenetrating and non-interpenetrating points obtained by ICP against our approach within a very low distance range $[0, 0.2]$ of corresponding points in the obtained registrations (Figure 3.8(c) and 3.8(d)). From the alignment obtained by ICP we sorted the points in A according to their corresponding point distance values in B and extracted the set U of non-interpenetrating points in A by the SIM calculation (the same was done for the alignment obtained by our approach). Given the position of each point in U we can verify, at the same position in the alignment obtained by our approach, which of these points are considered as interpenetrating points. Then, we can recognize those points considered to be non-interpenetrating in the ICP registration which are interpenetration points in the registration obtained by our approach, and vice-versa, as shown in Figure 3.11.

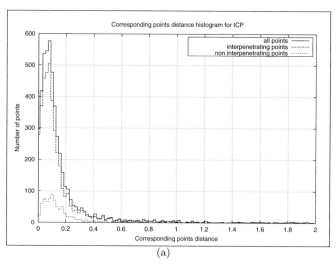

(a)

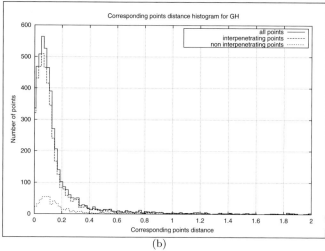

(b)

Fig. 3.9 Histograms using the alignments of Figure 3.8 with the range of Euclidean distances between corresponding points, set within $[0, 2]$ (a) for the alignment of Figure 3.8(c) obtained by the ICP-based approach using different MSE ranges; and (b) for the alignment of Figure 3.8(d) obtained by our GH method (see Chapter 4.10) using different MSE ranges.

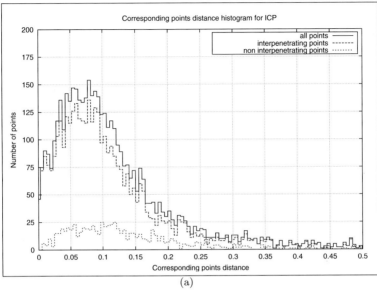

(a)

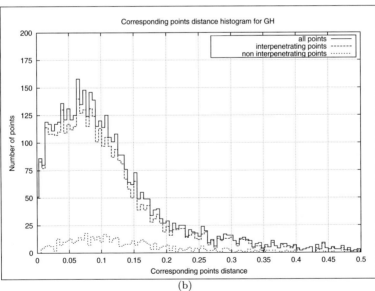

(b)

Fig. 3.10 The same histograms of Figure 3.9 but with the range of Euclidean distances between corresponding points, set within $[0, 0.5]$

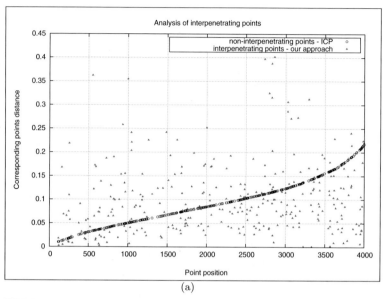

(a)

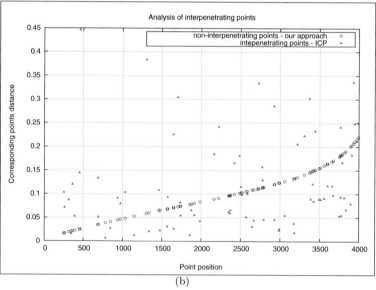

(b)

Fig. 3.11   Analysis of interpenetrating points between the alignments of Figure 3.8: (a) shows 395 points considered non-interpenetrating points in the ICP registration and interpenetrating points in the registration by our approach for the same point positions; and (b) shows 141 points considered non-interpenetrating points in the registration by our approach and interpenetrating points in the ICP registration for the same point positions.

We observed that the registration by ICP presents a larger number of non-interpenetrating points (280% more) in this low distance range than our approach. As can be seen, the registration in Figure 3.8(c) presents regions with a very low MSE but without interpenetrating points because in these regions the surfaces are parallel. In fact, the overlapping region between two aligned views must present a very low MSE between corresponding points, but if we analyze this alignment using the SIM, we can identify non-interpenetrating points having low corresponding distance. With this we can use the SIM to guarantee precise alignments having low MSE and high SIM (see Figure 3.8(d)).

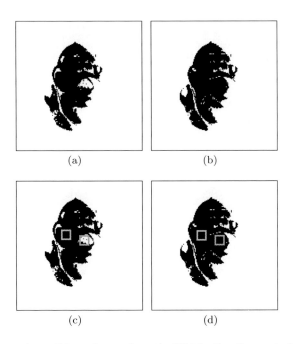

(a)   (b)

(c)   (d)

Fig. 3.12   Comparison of binary images from the SIM for the alignment of Figure 3.8(c) and 3.8(d) on different regions: (a) and (b) are the previous results of Figures 3.8(g) and 3.8(h), respectively; (c) within the left box the MSE= 0.062905 and within the right box the MSE= 0.137839; (d) within the left box the MSE= 0.063036 and within right box the MSE= 0.093385.

We also observed for several alignments that in some regions the error can be very low while in others the error can be significantly higher. This effect can be seen in Figure 3.8(g) (see page 26) in which the binary image of the SIM presents some "gaps", because in these regions the surfaces are parallel and there is no interpenetration. We computed the MSE over different regions for both correct alignments of Figure 3.8. For example, Figure 3.12 shows two regions for visual analysis. The MSE in the region of the left box is not significantly lower for ICP because in this region the alignment between the surfaces is very close. In the region of the right box the ICP result is significantly different than ours because there is no interpenetration; the surfaces are parallel. In fact, the variation in the MSE for our approach over different regions of the surface is less meaningful than for the ICP because we do not rely on MSE alone.

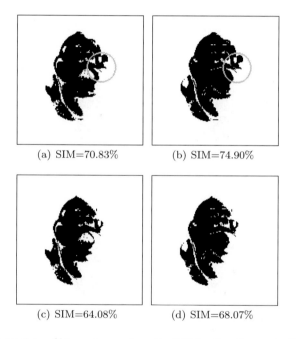

(a) SIM=70.83%   (b) SIM=74.90%

(c) SIM=64.08%   (d) SIM=68.07%

Fig. 3.13   Comparison of binary images from the SIM for the alignment of Figure 3.8(c) and 3.8(d): (a) and (b) are the previous results of Figures 3.8(g) and 3.8(h), respectively; (c) and (d) results obtained by applying constraint cs_1 on (a) and (b), respectively. As can be seen in (c) and (d), on the right side of the object (marked with circles) some false interpenetrating points were eliminated since there is no overlap in this area because of occlusion (please, see Figures 3.8(a) and 3.8(b) in page 26).

We analyzed the MSE and SIM, applying restrictions in the process measurement to correspond to the ICP-based approach used in our experiments. Specifically, we eliminated corresponding points on the boundary of the surfaces (constraint cs_1). By using constraint cs_1, the SIM and

MSE results for Figure 3.8 are: (c) MSE= 0.2539 and SIM= 64.08%; (d) MSE= 0.2546 and SIM= 68.07%. Even with this constraint the results were favorable and again, the SIM is more discriminating than the MSE. Additionally, cs_1 is very efficient at avoiding erroneous correspondences and in the SIM it also served to eliminate false interpenetrating points, as shown in Figure 3.13. The graphic in Figure 3.14 shows the results of the SIM by using constraint cs_1 as an improvement for the same classification presented previously in Figure 3.6.

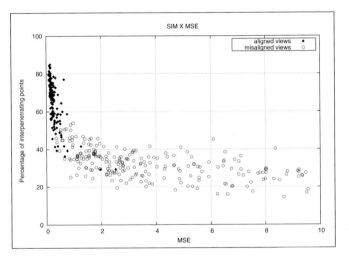

Fig. 3.14   Results for 496 classified alignments as presented previously in Figure 3.6 but using constraint cs_1 to compute the SIM. Now we can more reliably identify a good alignment with a low MSE and a high SIM.

By using only the interpenetrating points to compute the MSE we observed that the alignment obtained by our approach, which uses the SIM as a measure in the registration process, preserves a low inter-point error. The results of MSE only in the interpenetrating points for Figure 3.8 are: (c) MSE= 0.6368 and (d) MSE= 0.5789. Even when the MSE is computed for the interpenetrating points and its neighbors (8-connected pixels) the SIM results are favorable: (c) MSE=0.9203 and (d) MSE=0.8649. This result confirms that a better alignment can be obtained by increasing the SIM while preserving a low MSE. If we also apply constraint cs_1 in this MSE measure, the respective results are: (c) MSE= 0.25889 and (d) MSE= 0.24921; and MSE= 0.26141 and (d) MSE= 0.25775 when including interpenetrating and neighbor points.

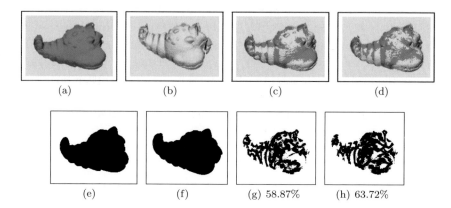

(a)   (b)   (c)   (d)

(e)   (f)   (g) 58.87%   (h) 63.72%

Fig. 3.15   Binary images from the SIM for the alignment between views (a) and (b). Figures (e) and (f) are the respective binary images of (a) and (b), which represent points in the surface of the object; (c) and (d) shows the alignment obtained by ICP and by our developed GA method, respectively; (g) and (h) the SIM of the alignments in (c) and (d), respectively with (f) as A in the SIM calculation.

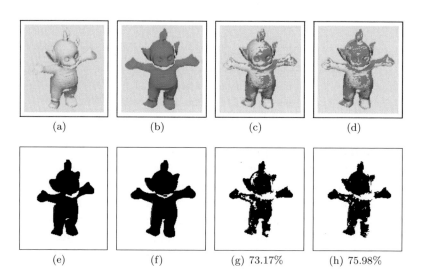

(a)   (b)   (c)   (d)

(e)   (f)   (g) 73.17%   (h) 75.98%

Fig. 3.16   Binary images from the SIM for the alignment between views (a) and (b). Figures (e) and (f) are the respective binary images of (a) and (b), which represent points in the surface of the object; (c) and (d) shows the alignment obtained by ICP and by our developed GA method, respectively; (g) and (h) the SIM of the alignments in (c) and (d), respectively with (f) as A in the SIM calculation.

Figures 3.15 and 3.16 show another two examples of correct registration to compare the MSE and SIM values. For both examples the SIM was calculated by using constraint cs_1. The results for Figure 3.15 are: (c) MSE= 0.4454 and (d) MSE= 0.4923; and (c) MSE= 0.4356 and (d) MSE= 0.3871 for MSE computed only with the interpenetrating points. The results for Figure 3.16 are: (c) MSE= 0.1794 and (d) MSE= 0.1905; and (c) MSE= 0.11638 and (d) MSE= 0.11557 for MSE computed only with the interpenetrating points.

These results show that the SIM better distributes the error over the whole surface while increasing the number of interpenetrating points. We confirmed that the SIM is a reliable and efficient measure to discriminate precise and imprecise alignments.

3.3 Parameters and constraints on the SIM

The formulation of the SIM (see page 22) is simple, efficient and easy to understand. However, we can define some constraints to make the SIM more robust and precise. A good example was presented in Section 3.2 by using constraint cs_1 to eliminatecorresponding points on the boundaries of the surfaces.

We next explore different parameters and constraints to be applied to the SIM formulation and present a number of experiments to show its stability and performance. The set of defined parameters and constraints based on Eqs. 3.1 and 3.2 are:

- $\boldsymbol{pm_1}$: The size of the square window centered on p, which defines the neighborhood N_p;
- $\boldsymbol{pm_2}$: The minimum number of pairs of points in A within the neighborhood N_p and separated by the local tangent plane at c for p to be declared "interpenetrating", that is $p \in C$. In this case, $0 \leq pm_2 \leq \frac{pm_1}{2}$;
- $\boldsymbol{pm_3}$: The maximum distance allowed between a point p in A and its correspondent c in B. With this, $p \in C$ only if $\|p - c\| \leq pm_3$;
- $\boldsymbol{pm_4}$: The maximum distance allowed between each point $q \in N_p$ and the tangent plane at c. In this case, $q \in N_p$ only if $\|q - c\| \leq pm_4$;
- $\boldsymbol{pm_5}$: The maximum angle allowed between the normal vectors at c and p, $\vec{n}_c$ and $\vec{n}_p$, respectively. Then, we have $p \in C$ only if $\cos^{-1}(\vec{n}_c \cdot \vec{n}_p) \leq pm_5$;

- cs_1: Constraint to eliminate the corresponding points on the surfaces boundaries. In this case, $p \in C$ if $c \notin E$, with E the set of boundary points in B. We also can define the thickness of the boundary as parameter pcs_1, usually $pcs_1 = 1$ by default;

From this set of parameters and constraints, only pm_1 and pm_2 are used in the definition of the SIM in Eqs. 3.1 and 3.2. Based on our observations we set $pm_1 = 5$ and $pm_2 = 1$.

We observed that the size of the window, defined by pm_1, has only a small influence on the SIM for incorrect alignments, but may generate significant differences for correct alignments. Clearly the SIM was developed based on a local visual effect, the interpenetration of two surfaces. Consequently it is necessary to use a small window, such as 5×5, to effectively verify those regions of the surface for which interpenetration occurs. Furthermore, a large window may yield incorrect local measurements for correct alignments. By using as example the correct alignments obtained in Fig 3.8 we can compare the SIM results by changing the parameter pm_1 as shown in Figure 3.17.

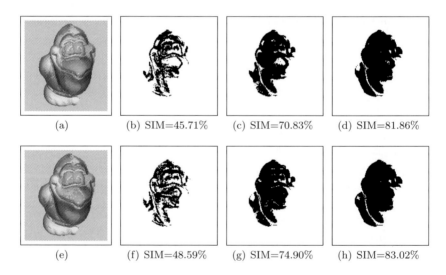

(a)	(b) SIM=45.71%	(c) SIM=70.83%	(d) SIM=81.86%
(e)	(f) SIM=48.59%	(g) SIM=74.90%	(h) SIM=83.02%

Fig. 3.17 Comparison of binary images from the SIM for correct alignments: (a) and (e) are the same results of Figures 3.8(c) and 3.8(d), respectively; (b)-(d) are the results of the SIM calculated on (a) with pm_1 set to 3, 5 and 7, respectively; (f)-(h) are the results of the SIM calculated for (e) with pm_1 set to 3, 5 and 7, respectively.

Figure 3.18 shows the results of SIM with different values for pm_1 for an example with an incorrect alignment. This example shows that the region of the interpenetration becomes thicker when the size of the window increases. This is to be expected because the probability of finding a pair of points separated by the tangent plane, as illustrated in Figure 3.4, is higher for a larger window.

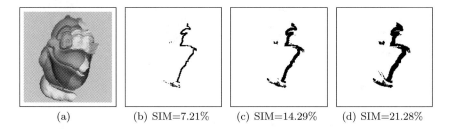

(a)   (b) SIM=7.21%   (c) SIM=14.29%   (d) SIM=21.28%

Fig. 3.18   Comparison of binary images from the SIM for an incorrect alignment: (a) is the visualization of the incorrect alignment; (b)-(d) are the results of the SIM calculated for (a) with pm_1 set to 3, 5 and 7, respectively.

In our experiments we verified that even with a very small window, such as 3×3, the SIM presents good results for correct alignments but usually some points were not included as interpenetrating points in small regions with low curvature. Because of this we decided to set $pm_1 = 5$ in our comparative tests.

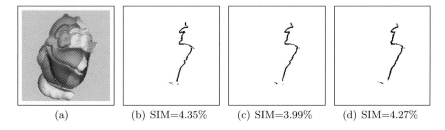

(a)   (b) SIM=4.35%   (c) SIM=3.99%   (d) SIM=4.27%

Fig. 3.19   Comparison of binary images from the SIM for an incorrect alignment: (a) is the visualization of the incorrect alignment; (b)-(d) are the results of the SIM calculated for (a) with pm_1 set to 3, 5 and 7, and with pm_2 set to 2, 8 and 17, respectively.

The parameter pm_2 can be used to avoid the "thickening" effect shown in Figure 3.18 when pm_1 increases. Figure 3.19 shows the results presented in Figure 3.18 added pm_2 with different values. Also, the parameter pm_2

can be used to ensure good interpenetrating points with more pairs of points separated by the tangent plane. Figure 3.20 shows the results for the correct alignments of Figure 3.8 obtained with $pm_1 = 5$ and pm_2 assuming different values.

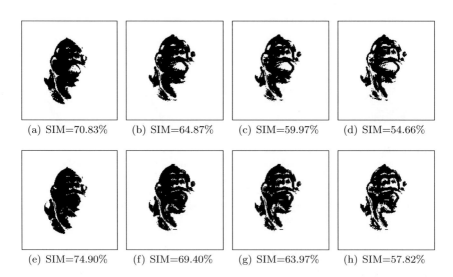

(a) SIM=70.83%	(b) SIM=64.87%	(c) SIM=59.97%	(d) SIM=54.66%
(e) SIM=74.90%	(f) SIM=69.40%	(g) SIM=63.97%	(h) SIM=57.82%

Fig. 3.20   Comparison of binary images from the SIM for correct alignments of Figure 3.8: (a)-(d) are the results of the SIM calculated for Figure 3.8(c) with pm_2 set to 1, 2, 3 and 4, respectively; (e)-(h) are the results of the SIM calculated for Figure 3.8(d) with pm_2 set to 1, 2, 3 and 4, respectively. In all cases $pm_1 = 5$.

After several experiments using different objects and databases we concluded that the SIM results using $pm_1 = 5$ and $pm_2 = 1$, and with constraint cs_1 provide sufficient discriminant information to refine correct alignments.

The parameters pm_3 and pm_4 can be used to make the SIM more robust in terms of precision. By setting low values for pm_3 and pm_4 one can avoid some incorrect measurements in regions with gaps or boundaries. Also, we can apply constraint cs_1 to discard incorrect correspondences, which exist between partially overlapping views. Figure 3.21 shows the results for correct alignments of Figure 3.8, including constraint cs_1 and parameters $pm_3 = 0.3$ and $pm_4 = 0.2$.

The parameter pm_5 can be used to confirm an incorrect alignment, such as that in Figure 3.18. In this example, the alignment presents a small interpenetration stripe in the crossing region between the views. However, if we analyze the angle between the corresponding points in the SIM we can determine if the surface is correctly aligned. Figure 3.22 shows the result by applying the parameter $pm_5 = 10$ in the SIM for the incorrect alignment in Figure 3.18.

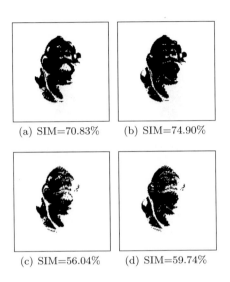

(a) SIM=70.83% (b) SIM=74.90%

(c) SIM=56.04% (d) SIM=59.74%

Fig. 3.21 Comparison of binary images from the SIM for the alignment of Figure 3.8(c) and 3.8(d): (a) and (b) are the previous results of Figures 3.8(g) and 3.8(h), respectively; (c) and (d) result by applying constraint cs_1 and setting parameters $pm_3 = 0.3$ and $pm_4 = 0.2$ for (a) and (b), respectively.

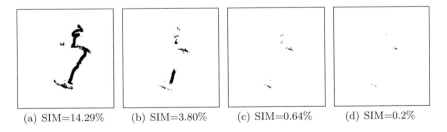

(a) SIM=14.29% (b) SIM=3.80% (c) SIM=0.64% (d) SIM=0.2%

Fig. 3.22 Comparison of binary images from the SIM for an incorrect alignment: (a) the visualization of the incorrect alignment; (b)-(d) results of the SIM calculated for (a) with $pm_1 = 5$ and pm_5 set to 25, 15 and 10, respectively.

Finally, we applied a full set of parameters to correct alignments (presented in Figure 3.8, page 26) to obtain a precise measure for the SIM.

Figure 3.23 shows the results of the SIM using constraint cs_1 with $pcs_1 = 1$ and the parameters $pm_1 = 5$, $pm_2 = 1$, $pm_3 = 0.3$, $pm_4 = 0.2$, $pm_5 = 10$. The MSE results are: (c) MSE= 0.2539 and (d) MSE= 0.2546. By using only the interpenetrating points to compute the MSE the results are: (c) MSE= 0.08854 and (d) MSE= 0.08728.

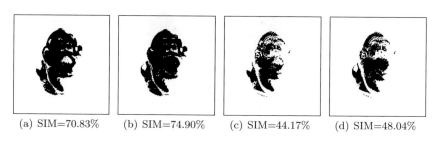

(a) SIM=70.83%   (b) SIM=74.90%   (c) SIM=44.17%   (d) SIM=48.04%

Fig. 3.23   Comparison of binary images from the SIM for the alignment of Figure 3.8(c) and 3.8(d): (a) and (b) previous results of Figures 3.8(g) and 3.8(h), respectively; (c) and (d) results by applying constraint cs_1 with $pcs_1 = 1$ and the parameters $pm_1 = 5$, $pm_2 = 1$, $pm_3 = 0.3$, $pm_4 = 0.2$, $pm_5 = 10$ on (a) and (b), respectively.

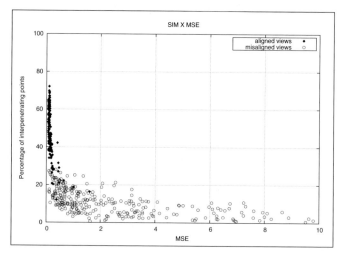

Fig. 3.24   Results for 496 classified alignments as presented previously in Figure 3.6 but using constraint cs_1 and parameters $pm_1 = 5$, $pm_2 = 1$, $pm_3 = 0.3$, $pm_4 = 0.2$, $pm_5 = 10$ to compute the SIM.

The plot in Figure 3.24 shows the results of the SIM using constraint cs_1 and the parameters $pm_1 = 5$, $pm_2 = 1$, $pm_3 = 0.3$, $pm_4 = 0.2$, $pm_5 =$

10 to illustrate the improvement over the result presented previously in Figure 3.6 (see page 24). We believe that a more exhaustive experiment using different combinations of parameter settings could provide a fine-tuned set of parameters based on range image characteristics for different range image databases. However, the current results for the SIM provide us a reasonable measure for range image registration evaluation.

3.4   Stability against noise

To show the stability of the SIM, we perform experiments on noisy surfaces. Given two registered views, we add to both views the same amount of noise and compute the SIM. This experiment was performed on several registration results and we tested different noise types and levels, that is, Gaussian noise, salt & pepper (S&P) noise, and a combination of both. The amplitude of S&P noise was set within the Z-values range of the images. In these experiments of this section, the noise was added after registration to show the stability of the SIM with respect to noise, for a given surface alignment. Registration results using noisy surfaces are presented in Chapter 3.5.

We observed that Gaussian noise has very little influence on the SIM of erroneous alignments. For correct alignments, *e.g.* Figure 3.8, the SIM increases with high noise levels. In fact, this behavior is to be expected since the apparent surface roughness increases with the noise, thereby increasing the number of interpenetrating regions.

S&P noise has greater influence on the SIM because many of the noisy pixels of one surface pierce the other, increasing the interpenetration even for erroneous alignments. This produces a significant increase in the SIM. To minimize the effect of S&P noise, we can introduce the parameter pm_4 into the SIM calculation. In our experiments, $pm_4 = 0.5$, representing approximately 1% of the range of values in these datasets, was enough to suppress the effect of this noise. Figure 3.25 shows an example of the erroneous alignment with different noise realizations to illustrate its influence on these images.

Figure 3.26 illustrates the behavior of the SIM with respect to noise level for a correct and an erroneous alignment obtained from a set of experimental registration pairs. In this plot we present three different tests: 1) Gaussian noise only; 2) Gaussian noise plus 10% S&P noise and 3) the same as test 2 but including $pm_4 = 0.5$ in the SIM calculation. This experiment shows that the measure remains stable under high noise levels (note the logarithmic scale). Moreover, pm_4 overcomes most of the noise influence. The experiment suggests that the SIM provides a robust indicator of alignment quality relatively immune to noise, sensor error, and other perturbations.

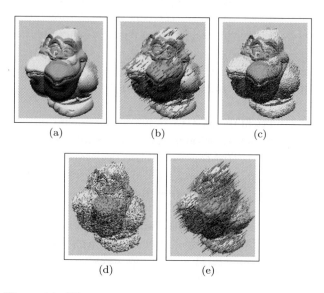

Fig. 3.25   Views with different noise types and levels: (a) initial alignment without noise; (b) 5% S&P noise; (c) Gaussian noise, $\sigma^2 = 0.01$; (d) Gaussian noise, $\sigma^2 = 0.1$; (e) Gaussian noise, $\sigma^2 = 0.01$ plus 10% S&P noise (with amplitude defined in terms of Z-values range of the images).

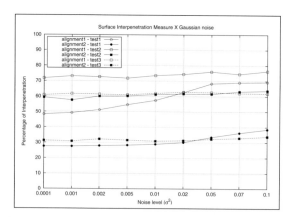

Fig. 3.26   Surface Interpenetration Measure against different noise levels. Alignment1 is a correct registration and alignment2 is an erroneous registration.

3.5 Discussion

The SIM, as we develop it here, presents an important improvement in evaluating range image registration, the identification of precise alignments. Experiments show that the SIM represents a more reliable measure than the MSE of corresponding distances. We observed that one can improve the registration by using the SIM while preserving a low MSE. By applying constraint cs_1 and other parameters we can better evaluate the interpenetration between different alignments and combinations of views.

We believe that is it possible to extend the SIM to deal with point clouds, representing surfaces in 3D, since some data acquisition systems do not provide the range grid. With this, we can apply the SIM to another set of applications such as remote sensing or robot navigation.

The experiments also suggest the combination of MSE and SIM to guide the registration alignment to provide precise alignments. In fact, one can define the range image registration problem as a multiobjective optimization process, in which the goal is to find the alignment that minimizes the MSE while maximizing the SIM. We explore this idea to develop a robust range image registration method, in Chapter 4.10.

Chapter 4

Range Image Registration using Genetic Algorithms

In this chapter we present the main ideas of Genetic Algorithms (GAs) as applied to the range image registration problem. First in Section 4.1 we introduce the concept of Genetic Algorithms (GAs) and their main strengths and weaknesses with respect to the registration problem. Section 4.2 describes the chromosome encoding for our registration problem. In Section 4.3 we describe a robust fitness function we have developed for the evaluation of alignments during algorithm convergence. Section 4.4 presents a number of experiments to identify a good set of GA parameters for the range image registration problem. In Section 4.5 we present different approaches improving the previous GA results, including the migration GA technique and the hybridization of GAs with hillclimbing heuristics. Experimental results show that by using the enhanced GA approaches we can achieve precise alignment within reasonable time. In Section 4.6 we present some experiments using different range image databases to illustrate the efficiency of our registration approach. A comparison between GA and Simulated Annealing (SA) for the range image registration problem appears in Section 4.7. To show the effectiveness of the approach in aligning low-overlap views, we evaluated a number of view pairs with different overlapping areas, as presented in Section 4.8. Section 4.9 discusses the evaluation time for the range image registration problem and presents some results using a parallel GA approach. We conclude this chapter with a discussion of results in Section 4.10.

4.1 Concepts

From their introduction by Holland [Holland (1975)] and popularization by Goldberg [Goldberg (1989)], the behavior of genetic algorithms has been explained by making reference to the biological metaphor of evolutionary adaptation, while they have found application as a general-purpose stochastic search method.

GAs are computational models of natural evolution in which stronger individuals are more likely to be the winners in a competitive environment. Besides their intrinsic parallelism, GAs are simple and efficient techniques for optimization and search. The main advantage of the GA approach for range image registration is that pre-alignment between views is not necessary to guarantee a good result. However, the GA is a stochastic method and generally time-consuming.

GAs have been applied to image registration problems in several areas, including remote sensing [Chalermwat and El-Ghazawi (1999)] and medical imaging [Ahmed *et al.* (1997)]. However, there exist many difficulties in developing reliable and automatic registration methods based on GAs to obtain precise alignment; this book addresses these.

Brunnstrom and Stoddart [Brunnstrom and Stoddart (1996)] proposed a simple method for free-form surface matching combining GA and ICP approaches. First, an initial alignment is estimated by a traditional GA followed by ICP refinement to obtain a final registration. Their results show that, in some cases, this method becomes stuck in a local optimum; the authors concede the need for some modifications to their approach.

Recently, an alternative range image registration algorithm based on a GA was proposed [Robertson and Fisher (2002)] using a parallel evolutionary registration approach. The experimental results show that the method better avoids premature convergence. However, while this parallel GA approach reduces the computational time, it does not yield improved solutions, because the inter-point error between aligned views is not· reduced.

The general principle underlying GAs is to maintain a population of possible solutions (individuals) encoded in the form of a chromosome (a string of genes) and to submit the population to an evolutionary procedure, until some criteria can be satisfied [Man *et al.* (1996)], or until a maximum number of generations is reached. Basically, GAs combine selection procedure and crossover, and mutation operators with the goal of finding the best solution to a problem. Algorithm 4.1 summarizes the basic steps of a simple GA.

In the evolutionary procedure, each individual is assigned a fitness value provided by a user-defined fitness function; the fittest individuals have a greater chance of being selected for reproduction. With the intent of creating better individuals, the crossover operation exchanges the genes of each couple of individuals selected for reproduction. The created (offspring) chromosomes, before being introduced into the population, may undergo mutation, a random perturbation, to enrich the genetic material in the population. Mutation occurs with a very small probability such that the evolutionary process does not degenerate to a purely random search. At the end of the evolutionary process, the fittest individual is taken as the final solution.

Algorithm 4.1 Genetic Algorithm

1: $i \leftarrow 0$
2: create the initial population $P(0)$
3: evaluate $P(0)$
4: **repeat**
5:    $i \leftarrow i + 1$
6:    select individuals for reproduction $\rightarrow I$
7:    apply crossover and/or mutation operations on I
8:    create the new population $P(i)$
9:    evaluate $P(i)$
10: **until** termination condition is met
11: **return** best individual of $P(i)$

The idea behind crossover is that the new individual may be better than either parents if it takes the best characteristics from each of them. Crossover occurs during evolution according to a user-defined probability and there are different strategies of crossover [Man *et al.* (1996)], including:

- One point: Randomly selects a crossover point within a chromosome then interchanges segments of the two parent chromosomes at this point to produce two new offspring.
- Two point: Randomly selects two crossover points within a chromosome then interchanges segments of the two parent chromosomes between these points to produce two new offspring.
- Uniform: Decides, with some probability, which parent will contribute each of the gene values in the offspring chromosomes allowing the parent chromosomes to be mixed at the gene level rather than at the segment level.

The mutation operator is an important part of the GAs to prevent the population from stagnating at local optima. Mutation also occurs according to a user-defined probability, usually set fairly low, and there are different

mutation rules. The best-known rules are the random mutation and mutation by range. The random mutation replaces the value of the chosen gene
(selected randomly) with a random value within some upper and lower
bound values for that gene. In contrast, mutation by range adds a constant
(user-defined offset), with the sign randomly chosen, to the gene's value
instead of replacing it.

To select chromosomes for reproduction one can use a number of
strategies, including roulette wheel, tournament, best and others [Gold-
berg (1989), Man *et al.* (1996)]. In roulette wheel the chance of a chromosome being selected is proportional to its fitness. The selection by tournament is one of the most used. Here, we apply the roulette selection N
times to produce subset of chromosomes that undergo a tournament. The
best chromosome in this subset is then chosen as the selected chromosome.
This selection method applies less selective pressure over than the plain
roulette selection. An elitist selection rule, "best", simply selects the fittest
chromosomes.

The population is usually initialized randomly. In this process, each
gene is set within a range of values based on the problem. At each generation one can discard a percentage of individuals (*e.g.* 90% worst individuals), based on a steady-state genetic algorithms (SSGA) approach,
known as the "elitist" approach. Another idea is to replace the entire population based on a generational replacement genetic algorithm (GRGA)
approach [Goldberg (1989)]. GRGA usually produces slower convergence
than SSGA. Using an "elitist" approach in the range image registration
problem, we observed improved convergence time without loss of population diversity.

GAs have been successfully applied to a number of theoretical optimization problems given the "building blocks" hypothesis [Holland (1975)].
The basic idea behind building blocks is that very fit individuals in the
current population pass on high performance features (substrings of the
chromosome string) to their offspring. Usually, chromosome strings with
a high fitness value must contain a substring that is a primary cause of
such a high fitness. Thus, even though crossover may split the string in
two, there exists a good chance that the highly fit substring is passed on
to the offspring. These highly fit substrings are known as building blocks.
Additionally, some genetic operations, such as uniform crossover may have
the disadvantage of destroying building blocks for some problems.

Despite their effectiveness, GAs are generally expensive to compute and
have many problem-dependent parameters to adjust, which are empirically

and carefully determined to avoid premature convergence. Since GAs can be performed using parallelism, many proposals for parallel genetic algorithms [Alba and Tomassini (2002)] have been developed to overcome the speed problem, but most do not improve the quality of the solution.

The setting of parameters, sometimes, becomes difficult and again is problem-dependent. However, there have been many studies related to this problem, and while the probability of crossover must be high the mutation rate must be low, as noted above, to produce a sufficient diversity of individuals in each generation. The PfGA (Parameter-free Genetic Algorithm) [Sawai and Adachi (1999)] attempts to eliminate the work of establishing the initial parameters for GAs. PfGA is a compact and robust algorithm that extracts one local population from the entire search space and searches the prospective space while varying the local population size adaptively along with other GA parameters.

4.2 Chromosome encoding

To perform range image registration using a GA it is necessary to define a chromosome encoding for the problem. Here, the goal of the registration problem is to find, in a huge search space of geometric transformations, a transformation T that can be used to align two views precisely.

As presented in Chapter 1.3, we can parameterize T with a vector $\nu = [\theta_x, \theta_y, \theta_z, t_x, t_y, t_z]$, where θ_x, θ_y and θ_z are rotation angles about the x, y and z axes (the X-Y-Z Euler angles) and t_x, t_y and t_z are the components of the translation vector. Then, we can represent the possible solutions as a chromosome string defined by six genes (using Real values) - the three parameters each of rotation (θ_x, θ_y and θ_z) and translation (t_x, t_y and t_z) relative to a 3D coordinate system. The chromosome's genes store the parameters of a geometric transformation that, when applied to one view, aligns it with the other.

To evaluate each individual of the population it is necessary to define a fitness function. The individual's evaluation is performed by applying the transformation T, obtained from the individual's genes, to one view and computing the MSE distance between corresponding points of the view pair, as in Eq. 2.1. To apply T to one view it is necessary to compute the rotation matrix R from the rotation angles (first three genes values in the chromosome). One can obtain the matrix R by multiplying the rotation matrices at each individual axis (R_X, R_Y and R_Z). Thus, $R =$

$(R_X \cdot R_Y \cdot R_Z)$ where:

$$R_X = \begin{bmatrix} 1 & 0 & 0 \\ 0 & \cos(\theta_x) & -\sin(\theta_x) \\ 0 & \sin(\theta_x) & \cos(\theta_x) \end{bmatrix} \tag{4.1}$$

$$R_Y = \begin{bmatrix} \cos(\theta_y) & 0 & -\sin(\theta_y) \\ 0 & 1 & 0 \\ -\sin(\theta_y) & 0 & \cos(\theta_y) \end{bmatrix} \tag{4.2}$$

$$R_Z = \begin{bmatrix} 0 & \cos(\theta_z) & -\sin(\theta_z) \\ 0 & \sin(\theta_z) & \cos(\theta_z) \\ 0 & 0 & 1 \end{bmatrix} \tag{4.3}$$

Given the rotation matrix R and the translation vector t, with $T = \{R, t\}$, one can apply T to one view and evaluate the MSE of the alignment as the fitness of that particular individual.

For most of our range image registration experiments we defined the range of possible translations to be half of the image size and restricted the range of rotations to within 90 degrees. To reduce the domain for translations we translate all the views to the origin of the coordinate system using their centers of mass. In Section 4.4 we explain in detail the setting of GA parameters.

4.3 Robust fitness function

To improve the GA performance we define a robust fitness function based on the sum of squared distances between corresponding points of two registered images. This function uses an inlier/outlier classification based on the MSAC robust estimator [Torr and Zisserman (2000)], and recently we successfully applied a similar fitness function to solve the range image segmentation problem [Gotardo *et al.* (2003a), Gotardo *et al.* (2003b)]. The MSAC is an improved robust estimator based on the RANSAC estimator [Fischler and Bolles (1981)]. The fitness value is obtained by the cost function f:

$$f = \frac{1}{N} \sum_{i=1}^{N} \rho(r_i) \tag{4.4}$$

where N is the number of points in image A, with $A = \{a_i\}$. The robust residual term ρ is denoted by:

$$\rho(r_i) = \begin{cases} r_i & \text{if } r_i < d \\ d & \text{otherwise} \end{cases} \qquad (4.5)$$

where d is a defined threshold and r_i is defined as:

$$r_i = \|b_i - Ra_i - t\|^2 \qquad (4.6)$$

where b_i is the closest point in image B to the point a_i, with $B = \{b_i\}$. R is the rotation matrix and t the translation vector, as given by the chromosome's genes. The threshold d defines the maximum distance between a corresponding pair of points to be considered inliers. The inliers are generally those points in the overlapping area of the aligned views.

With this approach we can find the alignment that minimizes the sum of squared distances between corresponding points while maximizing the number of inliers. Figure 4.1 illustrates the inlier regions of two different registrations with low MSE values. As can be seen, the alignment in Figure 4.1(b) presents more inliers than in Figure 4.1(a). The goal is to find the alignment having the minimum f.

In our current experiments we set the threshold $d = 5$ (approximately 10% of Z-values range of the images) based on the convergence results of different correct alignments, but we intend to investigate the possibility of automatically defining this threshold in a parameter-free version of our approach. We observed that a high d value may include some totally erroneous corresponding points as inliers, usually on the boundaries, while a low d value may reject good corresponding points, as outliers. In addition, the evolutionary process takes time to find good individuals with a very low d because most of the corresponding points must be in the inlier bound defined by d. Therefore, the threshold d is an important threshold to discard completely misaligned views in the evolutionary process while providing a reasonable tolerance between corresponding points for good alignments.

To reduce the inter-point error between views and, consequently, improve the quality of the alignment it was necessary to enhance the GA, as will be presented in Section 4.5. However, by using f in a traditional GA we obtained reasonable results even with low-overlap views. Section 4.8 presents experiments using views with different overlapping areas.

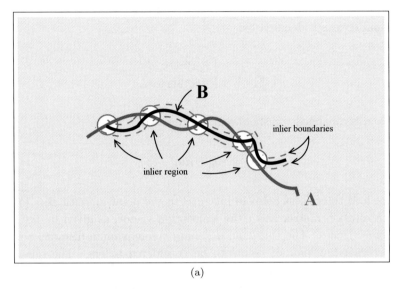

(a)

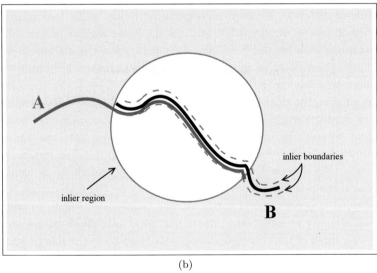

(b)

Fig. 4.1   Diagrams of different alignments to illustrate the obtained inlier regions, within the inlier boundaries defined by threshold d in Eq. 4.4.

We also performed several experiments with noisy surfaces to confirm the robustness of the cost function f and the efficiency of the developed GA approach. In these experiments different noise types and levels were added to both views *before* registration. Figure 4.2 shows an example of registration results obtained by our GA method using views at 0 and 20 degrees of the same object for different noise levels. The fitness values are: Figure 4.2(a) $f = 0.409$; Figure 4.2(b) $f = 0.422$; Figure 4.2(c) $f = 0.518$; Figure 4.2(d) $f = 0.733$; Figure 4.2(e) $f = 0.854$.

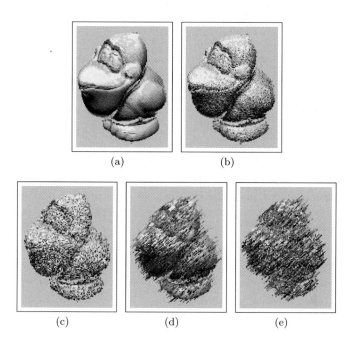

(a)   (b)

(c)   (d)   (e)

Fig. 4.2   Registration results obtained by our GA with different noise types and levels: (a) without noise; (b) Gaussian noise, $\sigma^2 = 0.01$; (c) Gaussian noise, $\sigma^2 = 0.1$; (d) 10% S&P noise; (e) Gaussian noise, $\sigma^2 = 0.1$ plus 10% S&P noise.

4.4   GA parameter settings

Because GAs have many parameters that need to be adjusted and they are generally problem-dependent, it is important to perform a parameter evaluation using different combinations to determine a reliable set of parameter values for a given problem domain.

Based on empirical results, we can define a good combination of parameters to apply to the range image registration problem. However, it is infeasible to test all combinations of parameters with different ranges - this requires an unreasonably large number of experiments. Some authors suggest the use of a GA framework to define the best set of parameters through an evolutionary process [Cinque *et al.* (2002)]. Thus, we confined our experiments in some comparisons based on the observation of other related work [Gotardo *et al.* (2003a), Man *et al.* (1996)]. By analyzing the experimental results, we can define a good default value for each parameter.

We can summarize the main GA's parameters as:

- Chromosome size, *chrom*: Defines the number of genes in the chromosomes (individuals of a population), which represent possible solutions. Here we set *chrom* = 6, three for rotation and three for translation.
- Population size, *pop*: Defines the number of individuals (population) in each generation.
- Population replacement (or genaration gap [Goldberg (1989)]), *poprep*: Defines the number of individuals of the population to be replaced in each generation. If *poprep* = *pop* one has a GRGA; otherwise one must have *poprep* < *pop*, which is an SSGA. The most used replacement strategy in an SSGA is to copy the most fit individuals to the new population. We set *poprep* = 90%
- Gene range, *generange*: Defines the range of values to which each gene can be set, *i.e.* the limits of each variable of the problem. One can set different ranges for each gene. For our range registration problem, the three rotation ranges are set within 90 degrees and the three translation ranges are set dynamically to within 50% of the image range (width, height, depth).
- Crossover probability, *crossprob*: Defines the crossover rate in the evolutionary process. Usually *crossprob* is set to a high probability, such as between 80% and 95%. By default *crossprob* = 90%.
- Crossover type, *crosstype*: Specifies how to combine the pair of chromosomes (parents) to create two new individuals (offspring). One can define different types of crossover strategies: one point, two point and uniform [Holland (1975)]. The uniform crossover has a fixed probability of swapping each gene of the parent chromosomes, usually set to 50%. We set *crosstype* as uniform.
- Mutation probability, *mutprob*: Defines the probability that a gene, randomly selected, will undergo mutation in the evolutionary process. The mutation rate must be low to avoid the degeneration of the population and is usually performed following the crossover operation. By derault *mutprob* = 5%

- Mutation type, *muttype*: Defines the mutation strategy. The most used are: range, constant, and Gaussian. For mutation by range, the gene's value is replaced with a value selected at random from *generange*. In mutation by constant, a constant offset is added (subtracted) to (from) the existing gene's value. Finally, in mutation by Gaussian, the offset value to add (or subtract) to (from) the existing gene's value is selected from a Gaussian distribution, usually with mean 0 and standard deviation 0.1. We set *muttype* as by range.
- Selection strategy, *seletype*: Defines the way individuals are chosen for reproduction based on their fitness value. There are a number of selection schemes [Man *et al.* (1996)], including: roullete wheel, proportional, tournament, probabilistic tournament, and stochastic universal sampling. By default *seletype* is tournament.
- Termination condition, *termination*: Defines the stopping rule for the evolutionary process. The default is to stop when the iteration limit *maxgeneration* = 200 is reached.

Our experiments were performed using four different view pairs (each one from a different object) from the OSU range image database, with views separated by 20 and 40 degrees. We computed the average fitness value of the best individual at each generation for all 20 runs of each view pair, *i.e.* the average of 80 registrations for each combination of parameters. Although we have used only four views to show a comparison of parameters in these experiments, we also perform a number of successful tests with different range image databases of different objects by using the best set of parameters obtained from this experiment [Silva *et al.* (2003e), Silva *et al.* (2003d)].

In the following experimental results we used their default values. Figure 4.3 shows the results for the comparison of a GRGA approach, *poprep* = 100% with different population sizes, defined by *pop*. We observed that a large *pop* value is necessary to obtain sufficient diversity in the initial population.

In our experiments SSGA with *poprep* > 50% is faster than GRGA and a large population is not necessary to achieve good results. If one has a large population, an SSGA with *poprep* = 50% suffices to guarantee good solutions. In general, an SSGA with *poprep* = 90% is a good option for different population sizes. Figures 4.4-4.6 show the convergence results for different *pop* and *poprep* values of an SSGA.

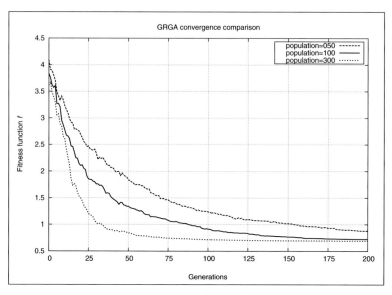

Fig. 4.3   Comparison of GRGA for different population sizes.

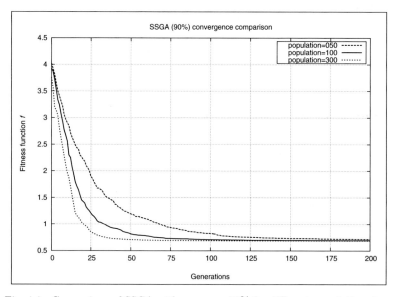

Fig. 4.4   Comparison of SSGA with *poprep* = 90% for different population sizes.

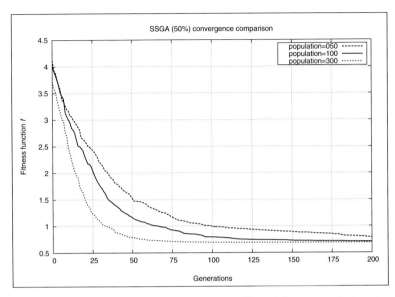

Fig. 4.5   Comparison of SSGA with *poprep* = 50% for different population sizes.

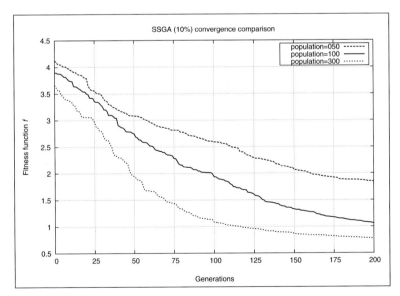

Fig. 4.6   Comparison of SSGA with *poprep* = 10% for different population sizes.

A combination of $pop = 100$ and $poprep = 90\%$ in an SSGA will reach much better solutions than a GRGA within 100 generations. Figure 4.7 shows a comparison between GRGA and SSGA previously obtained in Figures 4.3-4.6 with $pop = 100$.

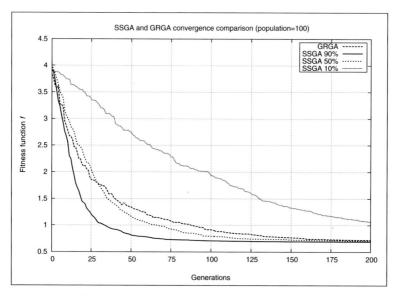

Fig. 4.7   Comparison between GRGA and SSGA.

For crossover operation, the results show that setting *crosstype* to uniform generally returned the best solutions, as presented in Figure 4.8. The analysis of each *crosstype* with different *crossprob* values confirmed that the probability of crossover must be high in the evolutionary process to achieve good alignment (see Figures 4.9-4.11). Finally, the comparison of the best combination results in Figures 4.9-4.11 is presented in Figure 4.12. One can see that the uniform crossover with *crossprob* = 90% returned slight better results. We observed at the end of the process *crossprob* = 90% is more effective at combining the genes of good individuals.

For the mutation operation, Figure 4.13 shows the results for *muttype*. Mutation by range returned slight better results. Figure 4.14 shows the mutation by range with different probabilities, as defined by *mutprob*. This experiment confirms mutation rate must be low (usually between 2% and 5%). However, if we analyze the mutation influence during the evolutionary process, one can see that it is most effective in early on. Section 4.7 discusses in more detail the influence of mutation and crossover operations.

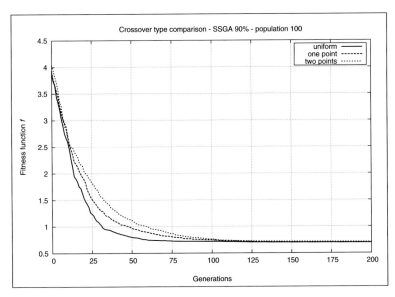

Fig. 4.8 Comparison between crossover types in an SSGA with $pop = 100$, $poprep = 90\%$.

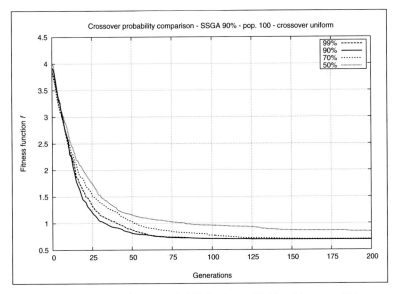

Fig. 4.9 Comparison of crossover probabilities in an SSGA with $pop = 100$, $poprep = 90\%$, with *crosstype* set to uniform.

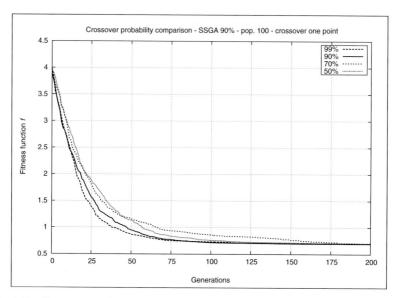

Fig. 4.10 Comparison of crossover probabilities in an SSGA with $pop = 100$, $poprep = 90\%$, with *crosstype* set to one point.

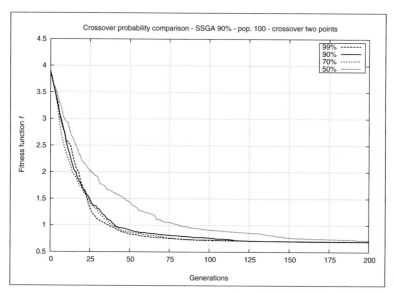

Fig. 4.11 Comparison of crossover probabilities in an SSGA with $pop = 100$, $poprep = 90\%$, with *crosstype* set to two points.

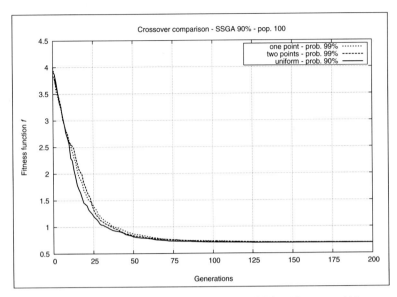

Fig. 4.12 Comparison of crossover strategies in an SSGA with $pop = 100$, $poprep = 90\%$, with $crossprob = 90\%$.

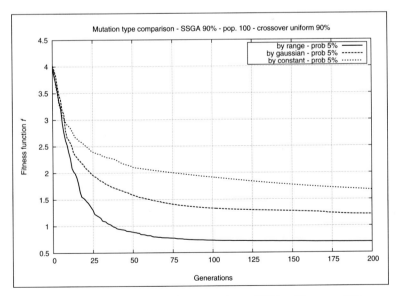

Fig. 4.13 Comparison between mutation types in an SSGA with $pop = 100$, $poprep = 90\%$. In mutation by constant, the offset is 1 degree for rotations and 1 range value for translations.

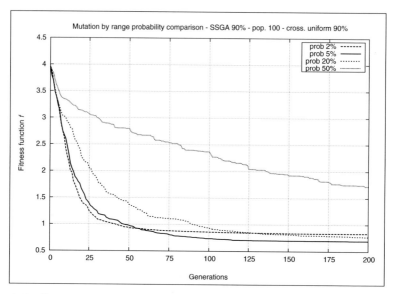

Fig. 4.14   Comparison of mutation probabilities in an SSGA with $pop = 100$, $poprep = 90\%$, with *crosstype* set to uniform and *muttype* by range.

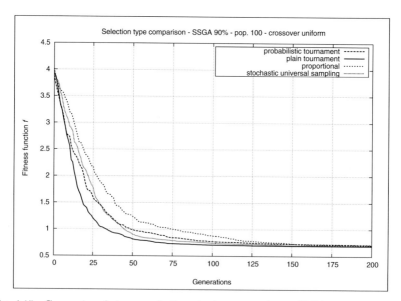

Fig. 4.15   Comparison between selection strategy types in an SSGA with $pop = 100$, $poprep = 90\%$.

To conclude the experiments we tested different selection strategies for reproduction. A number of strategies have been developed [Goldberg (1989), Man *et al.* (1996)] and it is essential to adopt an efficient scheme to effectively improve the solutions while preserving diversity in the future generations. Figure 4.15 shows the results for different selection strategies; the tournament strategy performed the best.

Based on these experiments we define default values for the parameters of our GA implementation as presented in Table 4.1.

Table 4.1   Default values for the main parameters of our GA implementation.

Parameter	Default value
chrom	6
pop	100
poprep	90%
crossprob	90%
crosstype	uniform
mutprob	5%
muttype	by range
seletype	tournament
maxgeneration	200

4.5   Enhanced GAs

The previous results (presented in Section 4.3 and Section 4.4) are reasonable. However, to reduce the inter-point error and, consequently, improve the quality of the alignment between views, it is necessary to enhance the GA. In fact, GAs are efficient at finding promising areas of the search space, but are not so efficient at fine scale search within those areas. In practical terms, *GAs can reach a solution close to the global optimum in a reasonable time, but a great deal of time may be required to improve the solution significantly beyond this point.*

In this context, local search heuristics such as hillclimbing can be combined with a GA algorithm to mitigate this problem [Renders and Flasse (1996)]. Hillclimbing attempts to improve the result by moving directly towards a better, neighboring solution, within a predefined number of attempts. We explored the hybridization of GAs and hillclimbing heuristics (GH) as applied to range image registration and obtained better results in far less time than traditional GAs. In GH, after each generation hillclimbing is applied to the individual with the best fitness value. Also, this procedure can be deferred until the evolutionary process has reached a good neighborhood of the search space, *i.e.* good solutions; the hillclimbing procedure spends much time at the beginning without significant improvement in the solutions. Thus, one can control the starting point of the hillclimbing procedure based on the convergence process, *i.e* when the fitness value of the best individuals shows only slight improvement over a number of generations. Another approach is to set large uphill offsets at the beginning and to reduce them dynamically as the GA converges. Similar to standard GAs, GHs can be implemented in parallel to increase speed. We outline GH in Algorithm 4.2.

Algorithm 4.2 Genetic Algorithm with Hillclimbing

1: $i \leftarrow 0$
2: create the initial population $P(0)$
3: evaluate $P(0)$
4: **repeat**
5:     $i \leftarrow i + 1$
6:     select individuals for reproduction $\rightarrow I$
7:     apply crossover and/or mutation operations on I
8:     create the new population $P(i)$
9:     evaluate $P(i)$
10:    apply **Hillclimbing** to the best individual b_i of $P(i) \rightarrow h$
11:    add h to $P(i)$ if it has a better fitness than b_i
12: **until** termination condition is met
13: **return** best individual of $P(i)$

In the hillclimbing procedure (see Algorithm 4.3), a gene from the best chromosome is randomly selected and an offset value is added to it. The offset is defined within a range of values, $[-c, c]$, where c is real. The result of the hillclimbing procedure is similar to "shaking" the alignment of views, seeking a better alignment in a predefined neighborhood of the best chromosome. If a better chromosome is found by the hillclimbing procedure, then it is added to the new population.

The offset value can be defined by a constant with the sign randomly chosen. However, our experiments show that neither very low nor very high values will improve the solution at the end of the evolutionary process. In fact, the effect is similar to mutation by constant, as presented in Section 4.4. Thus, we select the offset randomly from a range of values $[-c, \ c]$ and obtain much better results.

Algorithm 4.3 Hillclimbing procedure
___
1: $i \leftarrow 0$
2: set the maximum number of attempts max
3: set c value to the offset range, $[-c, c]$
4: initial solution s_0 receives the best individual
5: **repeat**
6:    $i \leftarrow i + 1$
7:    randomly select a gene of $s_0 \rightarrow g$
8:    randomly select an offset within $[-c, c] \rightarrow o_g$
9:    add o_g to the g value $\rightarrow s$
10:   **if** $fitness(s) - fitness(s_0) < 0$ **then**
11:     $s_0 \leftarrow s$
12:     $i \leftarrow 0$
13:   **end if**
14:   **if** $fitness(s) - fitness(s_0) = 0$ **then**
15:     $s_0 \leftarrow s$
16:   **end if**
17: **until** $i = max$
18: **return** s_0;
___

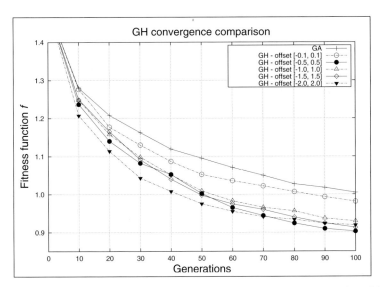

Fig. 4.16   Average of fitness function f obtained in the range image registration of different views within 100 generations using different range of offset values in the hillclimbing procedure.

We compare GH with the standard GA using different values of c and the averages of these results over multiple tests are shown in Figure 4.16.

In this experiment we computed the average of f values at each generation for 30 runs of each method using 5 view pairs, totaling 150 registrations per method. We set the maximum number of attempts in the hillclimbing procedure to 10. We limited the number of generations to 100 to illustrate the difference in convergence rate for each method. The other GH parameters are the default values given in Section 4.4. This plot shows that the offset range $[-0.5,\ 0.5]$ (representing approximately 1% of the range of values) provides the best results. A range of $[-2.0,\ 2.0]$ provided a good initial convergence, but no improvement in later iterations.

This experiment suggests dynamic settings for the offset range, which may take large values in early generations and then gradually be decreased, similar to the "cooling schedule" of Simulated Annealing techniques. We explore these ideas in Section 4.7.

We also explored Migration GAs (MGA) [Man *et al.* (1996)] to improve the solution and reduce computational time. The MGA has a parallel architecture in which the initial population is divided into a set of n subpopulations S by a master process, as presented in Algorithm 4.4. At the end of the evolutionary procedure, given by a termination condition, the master process receives the best individual of each subpopulation and returns the best of this set as the solution.

In the MGA, each subpopulation s_i is treated as a separate breeding unit, under the control of a conventional GA, as in Algorithm 4.5. The subpopulations evolve simultaneously (in different nodes of a cluster of n machines) and from time to time individuals are permitted to migrate among them. Each node receives its GA initialization parameters from the master process. For this experiment we used the Linux Beowulf cluster of the SAMPL at the OSU, composed of 6 nodes.

This migration process usually increases the diversity of each subpopulation (node), allowing better recombination of genetic material. When migration occurs, each node sends its best individual, while receiving the best from another node. This process is also influenced by the nodal interconnections, called the migration topology [Man *et al.* (1996)]. The migration topology is provided to each node as an initialization parameter.

In our experiments, migration occurs after every 10 generations and, for a better exchange of individuals, there is a link between each pair of nodes (*e.g.* unrestricted migration topology). The MGA obtained good (similar) solutions faster than the traditional GA. We also combined hillclimbing heuristics with the migration approach (MGH) and this method both accelerated the registration process and produced superior solutions.

Algorithm 4.4 Migration Genetic Algorithm (master process)

1: $i \leftarrow 0$
2: create the initial population $P(0)$
3: divide $P(0)$ into n subpopulations $\rightarrow S$
4: send each subpopulation of S and a set of initialization parameters to a distinct node of the cluster of machines
5: receive the best individual of each subpopulation $\rightarrow B$
6: **return** best individual of B

Algorithm 4.5 Each node of MGA

1: $i \leftarrow 0$
2: receive the initial population $P(0)$ and the initialization parameters
3: set the interval of time for individuals migration
4: evaluate $P(0)$
5: **repeat**
6:     $i \leftarrow i + 1$
7:     select individuals for reproduction $\rightarrow I$
8:     apply crossover and/or mutation operations on I
9:     create the new population $P(i)$
10:    evaluate $P(i)$
11:    **if** time for migration **then**
12:      send the best individual of $P(i)$ to other nodes
13:      receive the best individuals from another nodes $\rightarrow B$
14:      replace the worst individuals of $P(i)$ with B
15:    **end if**
16: **until** termination condition is met
17: **return** best individual of $P(i)$

To compare the four approaches (GA, GH, MGA and MGH), we fixed the GA parameters and ran a significant number of tests using views of five objects of the OSU range image database. We tested different settings of the GA parameters, such as population size, mutation and crossover probabilities, number of generations, selection rules, mutation rules, and others [Man *et al.* (1996)]. Based on the convergence time and quality of the solutions, we then fixed these parameters and ran a significant number of tests (since GAs are stochastic methods, conclusions based on a few trials could be misleading) to compare our different approaches.

The population size was set to 100 individuals based on our previous experiments (see Section 4.4). Small populations tend to result in premature convergence, while large populations increase the diversity but take time. The combination of 100 individuals and 100 generations consistently yields reasonable solutions. If the objective is to obtain a more precise solution, not just good registrations, one must increase the number of generations (in Chapter 4.10 we discuss the method to obtain more precise solutions). The range of the three rotation parameters (X,Y,Z) were set within 90 degrees and the translation values were set within half of the greatest image sizes (width, height, and depth). We also explored different ranges for the rotation parameters to analyze performance and efficiency. A range such as 180 degrees also provided correct registration results, but at least 200 generations were necessary to guarantee good convergence. However, we can safely reduce this range because the results show that the test image pairs were aligned with rotation never exceeding the range $[-45, 45]$. For translation we also observed that 30% of the greatest image sizes suffices to register the views.

In the mutation rule we choose mutation by range for improved genetic diversity. The probability of mutation equals 5% and the probability of crossover equals 90%. We selected uniform crossover and the selection procedure was the plain tournament rule. At each iteration we discard the 90% worst individuals, based on an "elitist" SSGA approach. GRGA produced very slow convergence and by using this "elitist" approach we observed improved convergence time without loss of population diversity. We applied each method 50 times for each one of the 30 test image pairs, six per object, and computed the average of the results in each generation. The average results of the fitness function f and the SIM in each GA generation are shown in Figures 4.17 and 4.18, respectively. We compute the MGA and MGH for 3 and 6 nodes in the cluster of machines. These results show that our MGA and MGH presented the best convergence results, followed by the GH approach. In fact, the MGA approach can be used to speed up the registration process. However, the quality of the solutions, as computed by the SIM shows that MGH and GH yield very similar results at this point.

In comparing the behavior of f vs. SIM-based convergence of the evolutionary process for each approach, we see that f provides a more effective measure of progress in the early stages, while the SIM is more effective in the "end game", as can be seen in Figure 4.19. This plot shows that early in the process, on the flat part of the curve, SIM is low and f is high. In this region, f provides a more sensitive, effective measure of progress. Later in the process, on the steep part of the curve, f is falling slightly while SIM increases dramatically. At this stage, the SIM provides the more sensitive and effective measure. Therefore, if both f and the SIM are combined we can obtain a more reliable registration process.

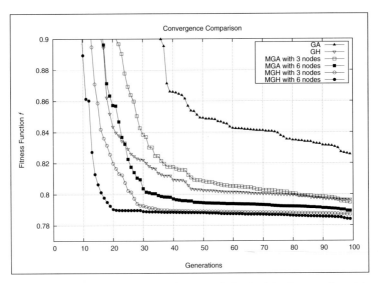

Fig. 4.17 Plot of average of the fitness function f obtained in the experimental results for different views of five objects.

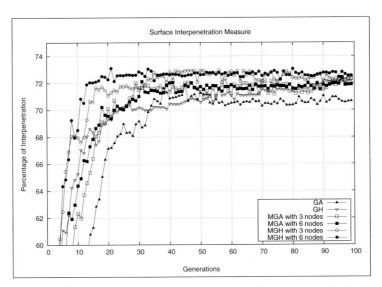

Fig. 4.18 Plot of average of the SIM obtained in the experimental results for different views of five objects.

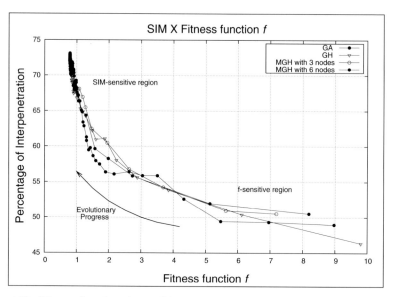

Fig. 4.19 Fitness function f vs. SIM measures obtained by the average results of different GA approaches to range image registration.

Also, we explore the combination of both measures SIM and MSE for further improvement, in Chapter 4.10.

We compared the GH method against ICP-based approaches based on the results of the alignment classification as presented in the experiments of Chapter 2.5 (see Figure 3.6, page 24). Figures 4.20 and 4.21 show an example (obtained from just one GH run) comparing GH with ICP results using the correctly aligned views of Figure 3.6, page 24.

We sorted the registered views by MSE (Figure 4.20) and SIM (Figure 4.21) values of the ICP registrations and compared the GH result for the same alignment number (see Appendix 7.2 for visual analysis of GH registration results). The MSE value was computed by excluding the corresponding points on the boundaries by using constraint cs_1 in the SIM. Figure 4.22 presents the same results as Figure 4.21 but using the alignment numbers sorted by MSE values of the ICP results, as in Figure 4.20.

The results show that, in general, GH returns good alignments with low MSE values comparing to the ICP-based method. Usually our approach achieves more precise results than the ICP-based method with higher MSE and lower SIM values. The alignments marked with **A** and **B** in the plot represent imprecise alignments with higher MSE and lower SIM values.

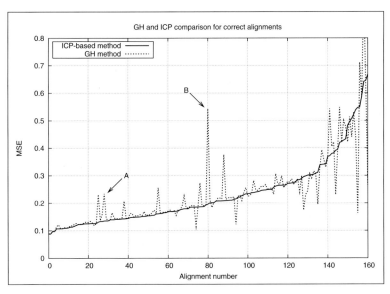

Fig. 4.20 MSE comparison of GH and ICP results for correct alignments in Figure 3.6. The alignment numbers marked with **A** and **B** in the plot represent imprecise alignments, but are not totally misaligned.

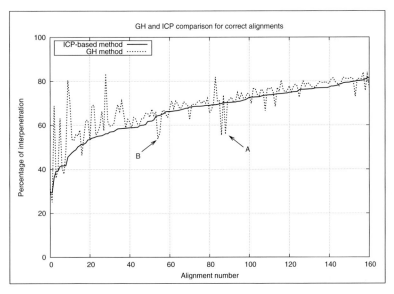

Fig. 4.21 SIM comparison of GH and ICP results for correct alignments in Figure 3.6, page 24. The alignment numbers marked with **A** and **B** are the same as in Fig 4.20).

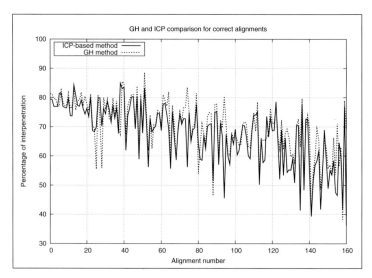

Fig. 4.22   SIM comparison of GH and ICP results for correct alignments in Figure 3.6, page 24. The alignment numbers are the same as in Fig 4.20

Figure 4.23 shows the alignments marked with **A** and **B** in Figure 4.20 and 4.21. Although the registration are not totally misaligned we observe they are imprecise because they present a low degree of interpenetration.

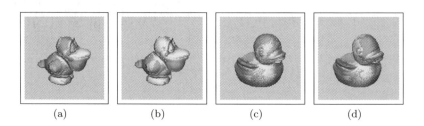

Fig. 4.23   Alignments of range views of two objects: (a) and (c) by ICP; (b) by GH method (see **A** mark in Figure 4.20); and (d) by GH method (see **B** mark in Figure 4.20).

Tables 4.2 and 4.3 present the relationship of the registration results in Appendix 7.2 to each alignment number in Figures 4.20 and 4.21, respectively. The characters "a" and "b" in the views' labels represent point-to-point and point-to-plane corresponding search in the ICP, respectively. For the GH "a" and "b" are the same view pair obtained with different runs of the method for comparison purposes.

Table 4.2 Relationship between alignment in Figure 4.20 and results in the Appendix.

Pos.	Obj.	Views	Pos.	Obj.	Views	Pos.	Obj.	Views
1	teletubby	20-0b	57	frog	240-220a	113	bird	320-300a
2	teletubby	20-0a	58	frog	160-140a	114	duck	220-200a
3	teletubby	180-160a	59	teletubby	160-140a	115	teletubby	60-20a
4	teletubby	180-160b	60	teletubby	160-140b	116	duck	260-240a
5	teletubby	280-300a	61	frog	320-300a	117	bird	100-140a
6	teletubby	60-40b	62	bird	160-180a	118	teletubby	60-80a
7	teletubby	60-40a	63	bird	320-340a	119	bird	60-100a
8	teletubby	280-300b	64	bird	220-240a	120	teletubby	60-80b
9	teletubby	320-340a	65	bird	220-200a	121	teletubby	200-220a
10	teletubby	320-340b	66	teletubby	260-220a	122	teletubby	200-220b
11	bird	180-160a	67	frog	20-0a	123	bird	180-200a
12	teletubby	160-180a	68	frog	80-100a	124	teletubby	120-160a
13	teletubby	160-180b	69	teletubby	240-260b	125	bird	300-340a
14	bird	80-100a	70	frog	300-320a	126	duck	280-260a
15	bird	100-80a	71	frog	160-180a	127	duck	200-180a
16	teletubby	180-200b	72	frog	100-120a	128	teletubby	40-0a
17	teletubby	180-200a	73	teletubby	200-180b	129	duck	100-120a
18	bird	280-300a	74	teletubby	200-180a	130	duck	80-60a
19	teletubby	140-160b	75	bird	240-260a	131	duck	60-40a
20	bird	160-140a	76	bird	120-100b	132	teletubby	180-220a
21	teletubby	140-160a	77	frog	280-300a	133	duck	320-340a
22	frog	40-60a	78	frog	140-120a	134	teletubby	100-80b
23	bird	100-120a	79	frog	140-160a	135	teletubby	100-80a
24	teletubby	260-280b	80	bird	300-280a	136	duck	240-220a
25	teletubby	260-280a	81	duck	120-140a	137	bird	280-260a
26	frog	220-240a	82	teletubby	200-160a	138	duck	320-300a
27	teletubby	300-320a	83	duck	140-160a	139	teletubby	260-240b
28	teletubby	300-320b	84	frog	320-340a	140	teletubby	260-240a
29	bird	100-120b	85	bird	160-120a	141	duck	280-300a
30	bird	300-320a	86	bird	140-160a	142	duck	300-320a
31	frog	40-20a	87	teletubby	220-200a	143	frog	280-320a
32	bird	260-240a	88	teletubby	220-200b	144	teletubby	240-200a
33	teletubby	240-220b	89	duck	200-220a	145	frog	120-100b
34	frog	220-200a	90	teletubby	220-240b	146	bird	320-280a
35	bird	240-220a	91	teletubby	220-240a	147	duck	160-180a
36	frog	200-220a	92	frog	260-280a	148	frog	340-300a
37	teletubby	240-220a	93	frog	180-200a	149	teletubby	80-100b
38	frog	200-180a	94	frog	120-100a	150	teletubby	100-140a
39	bird	20-0a	95	bird	100-80b	151	bird	120-160a
40	bird	260-280a	96	frog	60-80a	152	teletubby	200-240a
41	bird	20-0b	97	frog	280-260a	153	duck	20-0a
42	bird	80-120a	98	duck	180-200a	154	bird	340-300a
43	bird	120-140a	99	frog	120-140a	155	frog	160-120a
44	bird	140-120a	100	frog	300-280a	156	frog	160-140b
45	teletubby	40-20a	101	teletubby	40-60b	157	teletubby	120-80a
46	teletubby	40-20b	102	duck	220-240a	158	teletubby	80-100a
47	frog	240-260a	103	teletubby	300-340a	159	duck	300-280a
48	bird	200-180a	104	teletubby	80-60b	160	bird	60-80a
49	teletubby	180-140a	105	teletubby	300-280b	161	duck	240-260a
50	bird	40-20a	106	teletubby	300-280a	162	frog	100-140a
51	teletubby	320-300b	107	frog	100-80a	163	duck	260-280a
52	teletubby	120-100a	108	teletubby	220-180a	164	bird	160-200a
53	frog	260-240a	109	teletubby	160-200a	165	duck	280-240a
54	teletubby	140-180a	110	bird	40-0a	166	duck	300-260a
55	frog	180-160a	111	teletubby	280-260a			
56	teletubby	120-140a	112	teletubby	280-260b			

Table 4.3   Relationship between alignment in Figure 4.21 and results in the Appendix.

Pos.	Obj.	Views	Pos.	Obj.	Views	Pos.	Obj.	Views
1	duck	280-240a	57	frog	280-300a	113	teletubby	280-260a
2	duck	300-260a	58	teletubby	120-160a	114	teletubby	280-260b
3	duck	240-260a	59	teletubby	60-20a	115	bird	220-240a
4	duck	260-280a	60	teletubby	80-60b	116	frog	160-180a
5	duck	300-320a	61	teletubby	40-0a	117	bird	160-140a
6	duck	240-220a	62	frog	80-100a	118	frog	40-20a
7	bird	160-200a	63	bird	60-100a	119	teletubby	160-140b
8	duck	300-280a	64	frog	100-80a	120	teletubby	160-140a
9	duck	160-180a	65	frog	120-100a	121	teletubby	220-240b
10	bird	100-80b	66	frog	320-340a	122	bird	120-100b
11	frog	160-140b	67	frog	120-140a	123	frog	20-0a
12	frog	160-120a	68	frog	60-80a	124	bird	320-300a
13	duck	320-300a	69	frog	200-180a	125	teletubby	220-240a
14	bird	120-160a	70	teletubby	320-300b	126	teletubby	240-220b
15	duck	220-200a	71	teletubby	120-140a	127	teletubby	140-160b
16	duck	320-340a	72	teletubby	260-280a	128	bird	300-320a
17	duck	200-220a	73	bird	40-0a	129	teletubby	140-160a
18	frog	280-320a	74	frog	300-320a	130	bird	140-120a
19	bird	300-340a	75	teletubby	260-280b	131	teletubby	240-220a
20	duck	200-180a	76	teletubby	200-220a	132	teletubby	320-340b
21	duck	20-0a	77	frog	320-300a	133	teletubby	320-340a
22	duck	280-300a	78	teletubby	200-220b	134	teletubby	280-300a
23	duck	100-120a	79	frog	140-120a	135	teletubby	280-300b
24	frog	340-300a	80	duck	280-260a	136	teletubby	180-160b
25	teletubby	200-240a	81	teletubby	80-100b	137	teletubby	180-160a
26	duck	60-40a	82	teletubby	40-60b	138	teletubby	180-200a
27	duck	80-60a	83	frog	240-260a	139	bird	240-220a
28	teletubby	260-220a	84	bird	220-200a	140	bird	60-80a
29	bird	240-260a	85	frog	240-220a	141	teletubby	180-200b
30	teletubby	140-180a	86	frog	140-180a	142	bird	160-180a
31	teletubby	240-200a	87	frog	220-240a	143	bird	300-280a
32	frog	260-280a	88	bird	140-160a	144	bird	280-260a
33	duck	180-200a	89	bird	100-120b	145	bird	320-340a
34	duck	260-240a	90	frog	160-140a	146	bird	180-200a
35	frog	120-100b	91	teletubby	300-280a	147	bird	260-240a
36	bird	340-300a	92	teletubby	100-80a	148	bird	280-300a
37	duck	140-160a	93	teletubby	100-80b	149	teletubby	20-0a
38	bird	100-140a	94	teletubby	300-280b	150	teletubby	20-0b
39	frog	100-140a	95	teletubby	220-200a	151	bird	40-20a
40	teletubby	100-140a	96	frog	100-120a	152	bird	180-160a
41	teletubby	180-140a	97	teletubby	220-200b	153	teletubby	300-320a
42	teletubby	240-260b	98	frog	180-200a	154	teletubby	300-320b
43	teletubby	200-160a	99	frog	220-200a	155	teletubby	40-20a
44	teletubby	160-200a	100	frog	260-240a	156	bird	100-120a
45	teletubby	180-220a	101	teletubby	260-240a	157	teletubby	40-20b
46	frog	280-260a	102	teletubby	260-240b	158	bird	200-180a
47	teletubby	80-100a	103	teletubby	200-180a	159	bird	100-80a
48	teletubby	220-180a	104	teletubby	200-180b	160	teletubby	60-40a
49	duck	220-240a	105	frog	180-160a	161	teletubby	60-40b
50	bird	320-280a	106	frog	200-220a	162	bird	260-280a
51	teletubby	300-340a	107	teletubby	60-80b	163	teletubby	120-100a
52	bird	80-120a	108	frog	40-60a	164	bird	20-0b
53	bird	160-120a	109	teletubby	60-80a	165	bird	80-100a
54	frog	300-280a	110	teletubby	160-180b	166	bird	20-0a
55	duck	120-140a	111	teletubby	160-180a			
56	teletubby	120-80a	112	bird	120-140a			

4.6 Results for other range image databases

We applied our method to other range image datasets, including archaeological objects, historical statues and buildings. We used different range
image databases to test our implementations. Also, as part of the main
project of the IMAGO group, we intend to explore the characteristics of
many range image databases to provide more robust methods. Most of
these databases were created for cultural heritage conservation projects, as
mentioned in Chapter , page 6.

Figure 4.24 shows an example of our registration results using views
from the left ear of "David" statue by Michelangelo. The datasets were obtained from the Digital Michelangelo Project, Stanford University. In this
dataset we applied a sampling process to reduce the number of points, approximately 50%. The results of ICP without pre-alignment were erroneous
for this example.

Figure 4.25 shows alignments of views from the Thomas Hunter Building, supplied by Prof. Ioannis Stamos. Also, for this dataset we applied
a sampling process to reduce the number of points before invoking our
method.

Figure 4.26 shows an example of registered views from the Cathedral of
Saint Pierre, acquired and provided by Prof. Peter Allen.

Figure 4.27 shows an example comparing the GH approach with the
ICP on a dataset supplied by the Brown University SHAPE Lab. This
object was scanned in June 2002 at the site of the Great Temple in Petra,
Jordan, using a ShapeGrabber laser scanner.

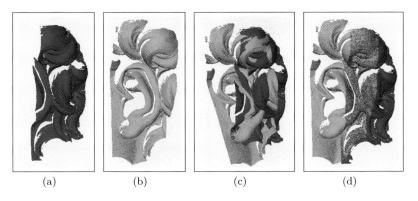

(a)   (b)   (c)   (d)

Fig. 4.24   Registration results obtained with an historical statue: (a) and (b) different
views of the object; (c) registration using ICP; and (d) registration using GH.

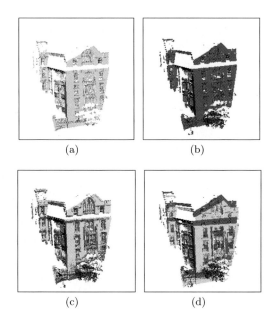

(a)   (b)

(c)   (d)

Fig. 4.25   Registration results obtained with an historical building: (a) and (b) different views of the object; (c) registration using GH; and (d) registration using ICP.

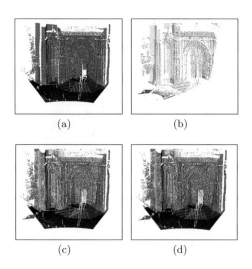

(a)   (b)

(c)   (d)

Fig. 4.26   Registration results obtained with an historical building: (a) and (b) different views of the object; (c) registration using GH; and (d) registration using ICP.

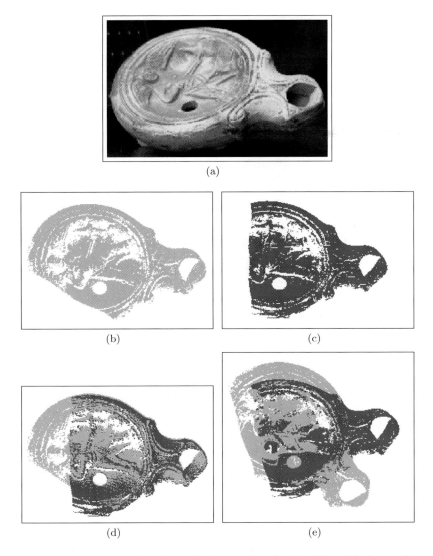

Fig. 4.27   Registration results obtained with an archaeological object: (a) picture of the object; (b)-(c) different views of the object; (d) registration using GH; (e) registration using ICP.

Figure 4.28 shows the registration results for an object from the IMAGO range image database. This object was acquired at a precision of 0.01 inches and each view has approximately 50000 points.

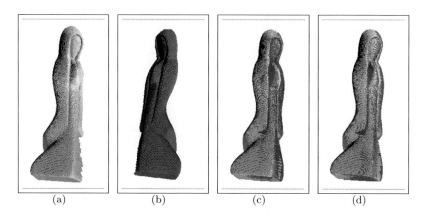

Fig. 4.28   Registration results obtained with an archaeological artifact: (a) and (b) different views of the object; (c) registration using GH; and (d) registration using ICP.

4.7   GAs and SA

Simulated Annealing (SA) is an iterative stochastic search inspired by the annealing of metals and has been used to efficiently solve many optimization problems from a wide range of application domains [Ingber (1989)]. Similar to the hillclimbing procedure in avoiding convergence to a local optimum, SA performs uphill moves with a probability controlled by a metaphorical temperature parameter (T) in an attempt to find a better solution. The probability of uphill moves decreases as T decreases. This process of decreasing T is called the "cooling schedule" and there are a number of strategies to perform this process [Ingber (1989)].

The main differences between SA and GA, from the GA perspective are: 1) SA has a population of just one individual; 2) because there is only one individual, there is no crossover, but only mutation operations in the SA procedure.

The goal of SA approach is to find a better solution by modifying the current solution with a local perturbation, since better solutions are more probably found in the neighborhood of an already known good solution than by randomly selecting from the entire search space. For some problems, evaluating solutions that are near an existing solution may be very efficient, which may give a performance advantage to SA compared to GA. However, the crossover operator of GAs is more effective at improving solutions because good local solutions in distinct regions of the search space can be combined to achieve better global results.

Additionally, SA has a fast initial convergence and obtains reasonable good solutions in a short time, but may not be able to improve on that given more time. In contrast, GA converges more slowly but is able to improve the solution consistently when given more time. Besides, the GA's convergence also can be improved with a combination of local search heuristics, such as hillclimbing, as we have already shown.

In general, SA is faster than GA-based approaches, but some works suggest GAs are statistically more effective than SA at reaching globally optimal solutions for a number of problems [Hart (1994), Youssef *et al.* (2001)]. We observed that SA is indeed the fastest method to achieve good convergence results. Thus, if the application demands fast answers, SA is the best choice. However, if the issue is quality, for example in the 3D modeling of archaeological statues, GAs may represent a better option.

We performed some experiments to compare our GH against a traditional GA and an SA method for the range image registration problem. The SA implementation was based on Ingber's work [Ingber (1989)] and the parameters of the SA used are the defaults of Ingber's VFSR library. We only eliminated the maximum number of times that the cost function repeats itself to try to prevent exiting prematurely at a local optimum. In this experiment we computed the average of 10 runs for each approach (GA, GH and SA) for range image pairs using the same cost function defined in Eq. 4.4. The comparisons are performed in terms of time and quality of the solutions achieved.

The results show that SA converges very quickly but that GA and GH returns better solutions. Figures 4.29 and 4.30 show an example of the results obtained in these experiments. Table 4.4 presents the cost values of the obtained solutions in each run to illustrate the improvements realized by GAs.

We also analyzed the influence of the mutation and crossover operations in the evolutionary process for our registration problem. At the beginning of the process, mutation is more effective than crossover, because the building blocks are not yet formed. However, at the end of the evolutionary process, crossover becomes more useful than mutation, because most of the building blocks are already formed and need only to be combined and that can be done efficiently by the crossover operation. Therefore, the utility of mutation at the end of the process is low and experiments with mutation alone show that it takes much longer to assemble these building blocks without using crossover. This can explain why SA cannot improve the solutions even given more time.

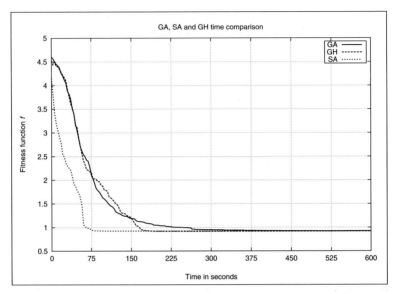

Fig. 4.29   Comparison of stochastic search methods in terms of time.

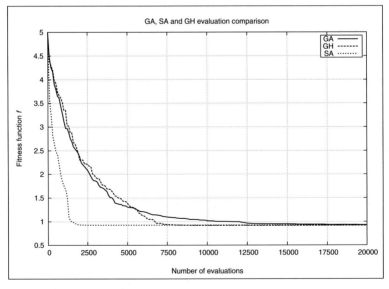

Fig. 4.30   Comparison of stochastic search methods by the number of evaluations.

Table 4.4 Cost value of solutions for SA, GA and GH for 10 runs.

Run	SA	GA	GH
1	0.926811	0.926424	0.918995
2	0.926813	0.925723	0.918651
3	0.926835	0.922001	0.918807
4	0.926810	0.920769	0.918647
5	0.926912	0.923867	0.918691
6	0.926818	0.922591	0.918646
7	0.922841	0.928005	0.918613
8	0.931059	0.924517	0.918841
9	0.926816	0.946007	0.918833
10	0.927034	0.923040	0.918920
Average	0.926874	0.926294	0.918764

Since SA and GA have different strengths and weakness, some work have has suggested integrating both into a more robust search technique [Cinque *et al.* (2002)]. First, a GA algorithm reaches good solutions, supplying them as input for an SA algorithm which can refine the solution to a better result. However, it is necessary to confine the SA search in a small neighbor area. In fact, this process is based on our GH approach.

We applied the "cooling schedule" scheme of SA in GH by generating a GH2 method in which the offset range is dynamically adjusted in the hillclimbing procedure. With this new approach we can obtain precise solutions in reasonable time. The idea is to compute a different c value for the offset range $[-c, c]$ automatically at each generation based on a function which represents a "cooling schedule". This function selects the c value dynamically within two values, T_{min} and T_{max}.

There are many different "cooling schedule" functions for different problems [Ingber (1989)]. We tested three different schedules, linear and exponentials, as presented in Figure 4.31. With G_{max} the maximum number of generations and g the current generation, to compute the constant c, with $T_{min} \leq c \leq T_{max}$, the linear $c1$ and exponential schedules, $c2$ and $c3$ are defined as:

$$c1 = T_{max} - g\left(\frac{T_{max} - T_{min}}{G_{max}}\right) \tag{4.7}$$

$$c2 = T_{max}\left(\frac{T_{max}}{T_{min}}\right)^{\frac{g}{G_{max}}} \tag{4.8}$$

$$c3 = T_{max} + T_{min} - \left(\frac{T_{min}}{T_{max}}\right)^{\frac{g}{G_{max}}} \tag{4.9}$$

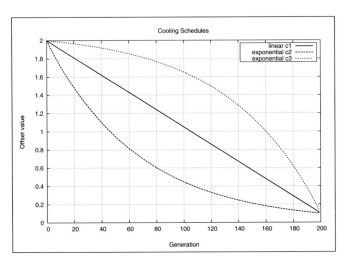

Fig. 4.31   Cooling schedules convergence with $T_{max} = 2$ and $T_{min} = 0.1$ for 200 generations.

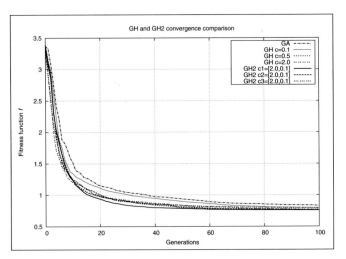

Fig. 4.32   Comparison of a traditional GA with our GH and GH2 approaches. The offset range is set to $[-c, c]$ and in the GH the offset range is fixed during the evolutionary process and in the GH2 the offset range is dynamically set by a "cooling schedule", with $T_{min} \leq c \leq T_{max}$.

We performed a number of experiments using different view pairs and the results show that one can obtain significant improvement in convergence time and quality compared with our previous GH results. Figure 4.32 shows the average of 20 runs for the same registration view pair obtained by the GH2 method with different "cooling schedules". By comparing the GH method with different range offsets as in Figure 4.16 we see that the linear schedule presents the best results, followed by the convex-upward exponential schedule c2.

We intend to explore the combination of SA and GA to create a more efficient and fast approach for archaeological applications in the near future.

4.8   Low-overlap registration

One the most important issues in the range imaging process is to know the amount of overlap needed between views to ensure correct registration. The acquisition process has a strong relationship with the registration method to be used. If a good relative pose estimation for the views is known (usually obtained by a calibrated system [Blais and Levine (1995), Levoy *et al.* (2000)], or by hand), the registration process can be performed using a fine registration algorithm, such as ICP. However, for many applications this method has significant limitations [Bernardini *et al.* (2002)].

Another approach is to have a large overlapping area between views to avoid the drawback of ICP-based methods, as done, for example in the Great Buddha project [Ikeuchi and Sato (2001)]. However, the acquisition process is time-consuming and expensive.

To overcome these limitations, one can use a robust registration method that can deal with low-overlap views and without a pre-alignment requirement, for example, our GH method. To verify the behavior of our GA-based approaches applied on low-overlap views we performed a number of experiments using views having different degrees of overlap.

Given a "ground truth" registration between two views, one can obtain different combination of overlapped views by simply cutting away parts of one view. By using "ground truth" registrations we can reliably evaluate the registration results. We tested three different methods to obtain the "ground truth":

(1) By using the same view to create the view pair. Different overlaps are simulated by cutting part of one view.
(2) By extracting two sub-samplings from a common view. Using distinct

sampling regions one can simulate different amount of overlap.

(3) By computing the z-buffer of the two rendering positions from a common view, in which the positions are set using known transformations. The overlap is obtained by eliminating the non-visible view's area in the z-buffer.

The main difference among these methods is that the views obtained with methods (1) and (2) have different sampling points in the range grids while in method (3) the range grids are the same. The experiments show that for our registration methods, which are based on pose space search, there were no differences using a specific "ground truth" method.

Based on this observation we ran a number of experiments using method (2) because it is the most similar to the real range sensing process. The overlap between views was computed by the SIM, with constraint cs_1, which avoids corresponding points on the boundaries. To simulate different overlapping view pairs, we applied vertical cuts in one view and excluded the left side of the cut, as presented in Figure 4.33. Thus, based on SIM values we define overlaps from 20% to 90% at intervals of approximately 10%.

Fig. 4.33   Overlapping areas for the same view: (a) 20%; (b) 50%; and (c) 90%.

We performed 50 runs of our GH method on each view pair with different overlaps. In this experiment we used the default GA parameter settings and the linear "cooling schedule" with $0.1 \le c \le 0.2$, as presented in Section 4.7. By visual inspection we identified the number of misaligned registrations and calculated the percentage of correct alignments for each overlapping area. Table 4.5 presents the results. We also ran the same experiment but using $pop = 300$ because some GH solutions presented a premature convergence for poor low-overlap view pairs. This improved the results, as shown in Table 4.6.

Table 4.5 GH results with *pop* = 100.

Overlap	Correct
20	68%
30	74%
40	84%
50	88%
60	94%
70	96%
80	94%
90	100%

Table 4.6 GH results with *pop* = 300.

Overlap	Correct
20	72%
30	88%
40	90%
50	100%
60	100%
70	100%
80	100%
90	100%

These results confirm that our GA-based approach is able to deal with low-overlap views without the need of pre-alignment as do range image registration approaches based on ICP. We intend to explore the limitations of registration methods applied on views having less than 20% overlap to develop a more reliable methodology for different applications, for example to guide the surface reconstruction of archaeological fragments [Leitao and Stolfi (2002)].

4.9 Evaluation time

Our GA implementation using the default parameters presented in Section 4.4 and the fitness function defined in Eq. 4.3 applied to view pairs, each one having approximately 10000 3D points, takes around 5 minutes on a 1.7 GHz Pentium 4 processor. We performed some experiments to reduce the number of 3D points by using sampling techniques [Rusinliewicz and Levoy (2001a)] to try to obtain fast results while preserving good alignments. The idea is to evaluate a small portion of points at the beginning of the evolutionary procedure and to increase the number of sampled points near the end of the GA process. Also, the same schedules presented in Section 4.7 can be applied to this process. We explore these ideas in a robust range registration method, combining the SIM in the cost function, in Chapter 4.10.

The evaluation process of our GA-based methods, which consists of finding the corresponding point pairs between views and computing the mean of their Euclidean distance, is very time-consuming. By reducing the number of correspondences searches at the beginning of the process, when the views are not precisely aligned, one can significantly improve the speed of the GH method while maintaining good results. Also, to speed up the correspondences search we can maintain a cache of corresponding point positions [Greenspan and Godin (2001)] over some number of generations, to be used as the starting point for the next search during the evolutionary process.

We tested different sampling rates and strategies, such as uniform, random and by normal orientation, as shown in Figure 4.34. We observed that uniform and random sampling returned better results than normal orientation. The normal orientation sampling concentrates the sampled points in regions with high curvatures, so most objects having large, smooth areas did not receive an effective sampling distribution. Thus, the registration results are imprecise when using normal orientation in the sampling process.

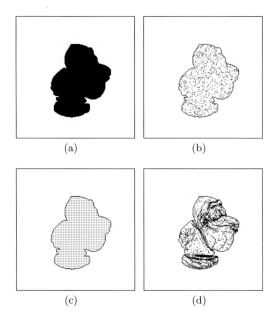

(a)   (b)

(c)   (d)

Fig. 4.34   Examples of sampling strategies to reduce the number of points in the range registration process: (a) point in the object from a range view; (b) random sampling with 15% of points; (c) uniform sampling with offset set to 3; and (d) normal orientation sampling with 20%.

The results with uniform sampling, with offset set to 3, eliminate approximately 85% of the points in one view to be align to the other view. These tests required 2 minutes on the average for range views from the OSU range image database using our GH method. In this case, sampling is applied to only one view (the view to be applied transformations). For this experiment, the number of attempts in the hillclimbing procedure was set to 10 and we used the linear "cooling schedule" with $0.1 \leq c \leq 0.2$, as given in Section 4.7.

It is well-known that the computational time of GAs can be significantly reduced if the process is performed in indexgenetic algorithm!parallelism parallel on a cluster of machines [Robertson and Fisher (2002)]. We performed experiments using the LAN/MPI[1] library on a small set of machines and easily reduced the computational time to seconds using GH. The main advantage of LAN/MPI is that it can be used in a heterogenous computing environment without any network or operating system modifications.

Although the main focus of this book is on the quality of the alignments and not on speed, we addressed the speed limitations of GAs and proposed some ideas to overcome these limitations. We intend to implement, in the near future, a completely parallel version of our methods for applications to a variety of range image registration problems.

4.10   Discussion

The experiments performed using traditional GAs were the first implementations in this book. Based on the first results we improved the methods and developed a new robust measure, the SIM. One of the most important observations in using GAs is that one can obtain reasonable alignment without requiring the pre-alignment needed in ICP-based approaches. However, it is necessary to improve the solutions to achieve precise alignments and to effectively compare the results with ICP. Thus, we proposed enhanced GAs to overcome this limitation and effectively improved the results in terms of speed and quality.

We explored a number of parameter combinations for GAs to define an effective set of values to be applied across different range views. This is a difficult task and some parameter-free approaches [Sawai and Adachi (1999)] may help in this process. We intend to explore this idea to create a more generic approach for range image registration. Nevertheless, the experiments show that one can obtain statistically good results with a fixed set of parameters, better than ICP.

Also, the problem of time-consumption was addressed in Section 4.9, although this is not the main focus of this work. Instead, we focused on

---

[1]http://www.lam-mpi.org

obtaining precise alignments to generate reliable 3D models from range images. However, we do intend to develop parallel versions of our methods.

Finally, these results guided the development of a novel robust range image registration method combining the SIM in the cost function Eq. 4.3, as will be presented in Chapter 4.10.

Chapter 5

Robust Range Registration by Combining GAs and the SIM

This chapter presents a novel approach for range image registration that combines GAs with the new Surface Interpenetration Measure (SIM). This approach is based on the previous results obtained using the SIM and our GH method, as presented in Chapters 2.5 and 3.5, respectively. First, in Section 5.1 we introduce the main ideas of this novel approach and define the cost function used in the evolutionary process. In Section 5.2 we present experiments comparing our this method to the previous results from ICP and GH. We also present an evaluation of our method to illustrate its efficiency in obtaining precise alignments. Finally, in Section 5.3 we present promising results using Multiobjective Evolutionary Algorithms (MOEA). The idea is to perform the evolutionary process using two objectives simultaneously, one to minimize the inter-point distance of corresponding points and other to maximize the interpenetration. We conclude this chapter with a discussion of the results obtained by our robust approach in Section 5.4.

5.1 SIM as fitness function

The behavior of f vs. SIM in Figure 4.19 (see Chapter 3.5, page 70) indicates that the SIM is a more effective measure than MSE for correct alignments at the end of the evolutionary process. Also, our experiments in Chapter 2.5 show that ICP results usually present fewer interpenetrating points than our approach, to be presented in this Chapter.

Based on these observations we developed another cost function g (see Eq. 3.2) to compute the fitness value of each solution. Because we cast GAs as a minimization problem in our implementations:

$$g = 1 - SIM_{(A,B)} \tag{5.1}$$

where A is the view position after applying the geometric transformation represented by the chromosome's genes. The fitness of the chromosome is given by g.

Clearly, the SIM cannot be used until the alignments are reasonable because it is not an effective measure of progress in the early stages (see Figure 4.19). We performed some experiments using g instead of f in our GH method and we observed that a great number of generations was necessary to guarantee a good alignment using only g as fitness function. We also explored combining both measures in a single cost function, $h = w_f f + w_g g$, where w_f and w_g are user-defined weights. By using both functions in GAs we can make the registration process more robust. However, a reasonable weight selection is not easily defined even through a normalization of the function domains. In general, one function will dominate the other during the evolutionary process and result in poor solutions, as reported in other optimization domains [Coello (2000)]. In Section 5.3 we discuss this issue and propose a multiobjective approach to overcome this problem.

Based on our previous results, we use f to evaluate the fitness of individual chromosomes early in the process. Later, as the surfaces become aligned, we switch to the SIM-based fitness function g, which is more sensitive and leads to more precise, robust registration in the end. We set a threshold n on the number of iterations to decide when use each cost function. It is also possible to make a switching decision based on the convergence rate similar to the "cooling schedules" of the GH2 method in Chapter 3.5. Here, the idea is similar to start two GAs successively: the first one uses f as the fitness function to provide good initial solutions to form the starting population for the second one using g as the fitness function. To reduce the search space and consequently increase the speed, one can delimit the range of gene values in the second GA since it is expected to begin with good alignments from the final population of the first GA. Furthermore, one can use the GH with g as the fitness function for range image registration refinements. This strategy is similar to perform ICP, a fine registration method, usually applied following coarse registration, as suggested by many authors [Sharp *et al.* (2002), Dorai *et al.* (1998), Blais and Levine (1995), Huber and Hebert (2003), Reed and Allen (1999)].

Our experimental results show that switching at $n = 100$ generations out of 200 generations in all was enough to achieve good convergence results using the fitness function f. It is important to maintain a high value for n to guarantee good solutions. Also, we observed that in just a few more generations the fitness function g can reach a very good solution by reducing the range of gene values. Our observations indicate that one can safely reduce the range of values to less than 10% of their initial settings and still guarantee precise registration. The results are presented in Section 5.2.

This novel robust technique was successfully applied to each of our GA methods, (*i.e.* GH, MGA and MGH). Algorithm 5.1 summarizes the robust approach using both cost functions f and g.

Algorithm 5.1 Robust GA

1: $i \leftarrow 0$
2: define maximum number of generations using cost function $f \rightarrow n$
3: create the initial population $P(0)$
4: evaluate $P(0)$ using f
5: **repeat**
6:    $i \leftarrow i + 1$
7:    select individuals for reproduction $\rightarrow I$
8:    apply crossover and mutation operations on I
9:    create the new population $P(i)$
10:    evaluate $P(i)$ using f
11: **until** $i = n$ (termination condition of a first evolution part
12: decrease the range for genes values (reduce the search space)
13: **repeat**
14:    $i \leftarrow i + 1$
15:    select individuals for reproduction $\rightarrow I$
16:    apply crossover and mutation operations on I
17:    create the new population $P(i)$
18:    evaluate $P(i)$ using g
19: **until** termination condition is met
20: **return** best individual of $P(i)$

5.2 Experimental results

In preliminary tests using the novel robust approach (Robust GA), we saw an average increase of the SIM of approximately 7% compared to the original GH and 14% compared to the ICP-based method. This experiment was performed using the original SIM without any constraint or other parameters, as presented in Chapter 2.5. We set the number of generations to 200 and switch the cost function when $n = 100$. Some tests show that ICP returns grossly erroneous alignments (*e.g.* duck 0-40, frog 0-40 and lobs. 0-40 in Figure 5.1).

Table 5.1 presents the MSE and SIM results obtained from different test image pairs. Note that, while ICP is driven by MSE, GH and the early stages of the robust GA are driven by the cost function of Eq. 4.4 and the latter stages of the robust GA are driven by SIM-based cost function of Eq. 5.1. In Table 5.1 we provide the recomputed final MSE, as well as the SIM, of each result for comparison. Although the MSE of the ICP results is usually the lowest, the views were not precisely aligned because the convergence was to a local solution. The SIM values of the ICP alignments indicate that MSE is not the best measure to guide the registration process.

To substantiate the numerical observations, Figures 5.1-5.3 offer a visual comparison of the registration results. These results prove that our robust approach using the cost function g at the end of the convergence process represents a precise measure of range image registration. Additionally, one can include another constraint in the cost function f, such as a limit on the maximum angle between the normal vectors of corresponding points, to improve the convergence of GAs in the initial stage, similar to [Gotardo *et al.* (2003a)].

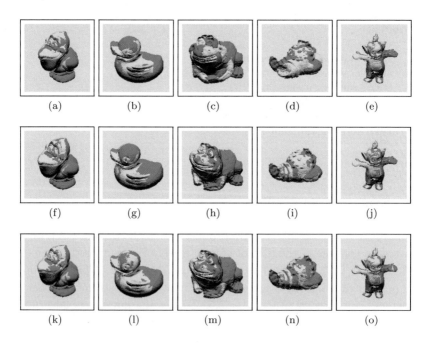

Fig. 5.1 Registration results of the test image pair 0-40 of the five objects used in the experiments. The top line are the ICP results, in the middle the GH results and the bottom are the Robust GA.

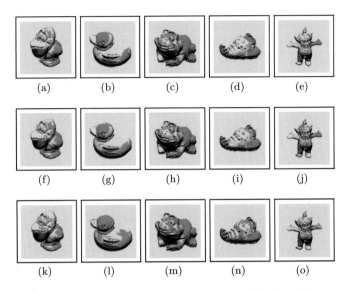

Fig. 5.2 Registration results of the test image pair 0-20 of the five objects used in the experiments. The top line are the ICP results, in the middle the GH results and the bottom are the Robust GA.

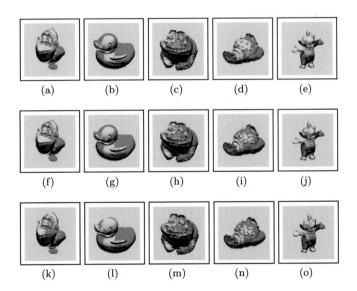

Fig. 5.3 Registration results of the test image pair 20-40 of the five objects used in the experiments. The top line are the ICP results, in the middle the GH results and the bottom are the Robust GA.

Table 5.1   MSE and SIM results. The first column shows the name of the objects in the OSU range image database followed by the view numbers of each test pair. The bold values represent grossly erroneous alignments obtained by ICP in Figures 5.1-5.3.

Test image	ICP		GH		Robust GA	
pairs	MSE	SIM%	MSE	SIM%	MSE	SIM%
bird 0-20	0.40	75.4	0.41	86.5	0.42	90.7
bird 0-40	5.19	52.6	5.55	60.7	6.01	77.9
bird 20-40	1.34	71.2	1.37	77.3	1.44	91.3
duck 0-20	0.63	43.5	0.65	46.8	0.80	57.0
duck 0-40	**3.28**	29.0	2.41	38.5	2.65	50.7
duck 20-40	0.86	43.1	0.90	46.1	0.98	56.3
frog 0-20	0.33	74.6	0.34	75.7	0.36	82.7
frog 0-40	**3.91**	36.7	1.92	64.9	2.03	68.6
frog 20-40	0.72	76.9	0.81	79.2	0.81	80.8
lobs. 0-20	1.06	48.8	1.07	51.0	1.25	60.9
lobs. 0-40	**35.79**	33.7	9.01	48.4	9.10	53.4
lobs. 20-40	3.30	53.2	4.00	50.4	3.95	55.9
tele. 0-20	0.22	82.3	0.23	84.8	0.23	91.0
tele. 0-40	1.36	67.7	1.40	72.6	1.48	76.8
tele. 20-40	0.43	82.6	0.43	86.5	0.44	90.3
Average	3.92	58.34	2.03	64.67	2.13	72.33

We also applied the robust approach to our GH method (Robust GH) and compared these results to those obtained by ICP in alignment classification as presented in the experiments of Chapter 2.5 (see Figure 3.6, page 24). In this experiment we set the number of generations to 200, switched the cost function at $n = 100$, and obtained very precise alignments. The results show that one can obtain precise alignments with this technique far superior to ICP-based approaches or even our GH method.

Figures 5.4 and 5.5 show an example (obtained from just one GH run) comparing the Robust GH and ICP results using the correctly aligned views of Figure 3.6, page 24. To compare the results with those presented in Chapter 3.5 in Figures 4.20-4.22, we also sorted the registered views by MSE and SIM values of the ICP registrations. We observed in Figures 5.4 and 5.5 that our robust approach presents higher interpenetration while preserving low MSE values. The registration results show superior alignments as compared with ICP-based approach.

In Appendix 7.2 we include all the registration results with their respective alignment numbers for visual analysis. The MSE value was computed by excluding the corresponding points on the boundaries of the aligned views by using constraint cs_1 in the SIM. Figure 5.6 presents the same results as Figure 5.5 but using the alignment numbers sorted by MSE values from ICP, as in Figure 5.4. The alignment numbers are the same as in the previous comparison, as given in Tables 4.2 and 4.3 (see pages 73 and 74).

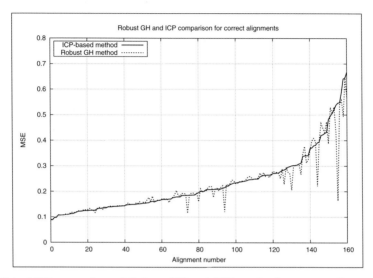

Fig. 5.4   MSE comparison of Robust GH and ICP results for correct alignments in Figure 3.6, page 24.

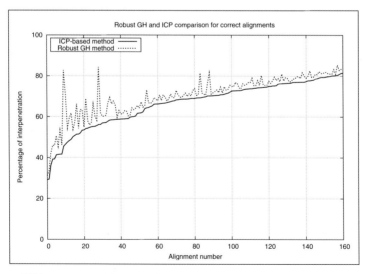

Fig. 5.5   SIM comparison of Robust GH and ICP results for correct alignments in Figure 3.6, page 24.

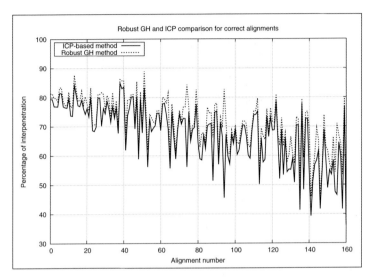

Fig. 5.6   SIM comparison of Robust GH and ICP results for correct alignments in Figure 3.6, page 24. The alignment numbers are the same as in Fig 5.4

Figures 5.7 and 5.8 illustrate the improvement we obtain with this technique. The registration results are shown in Figure 5.7 and their interpenetration binary images in Figure 5.8. Figure 5.7(b) shows the registration obtained by the ICP [Besl and McKay (1992)]. While this is a reasonable alignment, Figure 5.8(b) shows that there exists a large area with no interpenetration.

The result of GH (Figure 5.7(c) and Figure 5.8(c)) shows a superior alignment with more interpenetrating points. Following the suggestion in [Robertson and Fisher (2002)], we applied ICP to the GA results in trying to improve the alignment. However, the ICP met a local minimum and the results show that it was inadequate for this purpose. The results of our technique show the best convergence results and greatest SIM values.

The MSE and SIM (using constraint cs_1) of the registration results in Figure 5.7 are: Figure 5.7(a) MSE= 13.386 and SIM= 28.41%; Figure 5.7(b) MSE= 0.1509 and SIM= 71.37%; Figure 5.7(c) MSE= 0.1441 and SIM= 81.90%; Figure 5.7(d) MSE= 0.1429 and SIM= 85.42%; Figure 5.7(e) MSE= 0.1447 and **SIM = 86.05%**.

It is important to note that the binary images of interpenetration points (Figures 5.8(a)-5.8(e)) show better homogeneity in distribution when a high interpenetration value is found, proving the effectiveness of the measure.

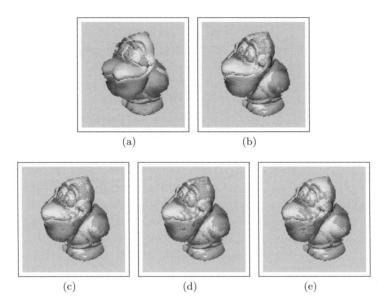

Fig. 5.7   Registration results: (a) initial views (0 and 20 degrees of a same object); (b) ICP; (c) GH; (d) GH+ICP; (e) robust GH approach developed in this book.

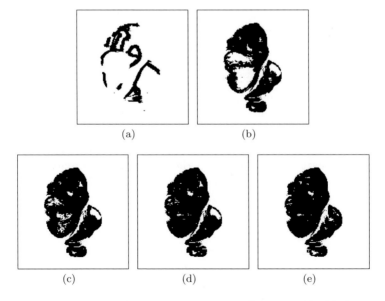

Fig. 5.8   Binary images of the interpenetrating points (represented by black region) of each registration results in Figure 5.7(a)-5.7(e), respectively.

5.3   Multiobjective Evolutionary Algorithms

For multiobjective search and optimization, evolutionary algorithms (EA) have been used effectively to handle complex problems [Deb (2001)]. Because multiple individuals can search for multiple solutions in parallel, these methods take advantage of any similarities available in the candidate solutions. Compared to traditional mathematical programming techniques, which require a number of separate attempts to obtain a set of candidate solutions, the multiobjective evolutionary algorithms (MOEAs) can reach the set of optimal solutions in a single run. Furthermore, in recent years a number of potential strategies have been developed that lead to promising results, including Co-evolutionary Genetic Algorithms [Lohn *et al.* (2002)].

A traditional approach to solving multiobjective problems is to combine all the objectives into one using weight values for each objective. This is known as the aggregation-based technique [Coello (2000)]. The difficult part of this approach is to define accurate scalar information on the range of the objectives and the weight values to avoid dominance by one objective.

To overcome the difficulties of the aggregating approaches, some of the most popular MOEAs use additional parameters, such as constraints (*i.e.* criterion-based technique). The main advantages of these methods are efficiency and simplicity, but they are problem-dependent and have intricate details, requiring empirical fine tuning of the parameters [Coello (2000)].

Recently, a number of multiobjective evolutionary algorithms (MOEAs) have been devised to solve different multiobjective optimization problems [Zitzler *et al.* (2002), Deb *et al.* (2002), Coello (2000)] without the drawbacks of traditional approaches. In general, MOEAs deal with different objectives (possibly conflicting) simultaneously and rarely a single solution is found as the result [Coello (2000)]. In a set of possible solutions one can define the best subset, known as Pareto-optimal[1]. These solutions are not dominated by any other in the search space (Pareto-based technique). The non-dominated (Pareto-optimal) solutions lie on the convex hull of the set of solutions in search space. They are confined to that part the convex hull "facing" the ideal solution. Any solution on this part of the hull will be better than any other other solution in at least one dimension.

Figure 5.9 illustrates the concept of Pareto optimality for a problem with two objectives, represented by functions f_1 and f_2, and assuming that functions are to be minimized. Pareto-optimal solutions are those solutions

---

[1]The concept of Pareto-optimal was formulated by economist Vilfredo Pareto in the 19th century, and is the origin of research in multiobjective optimization.

within the search space whose corresponding objective vector components (*i.e.* chromosome's genes) cannot be simultaneously improved.

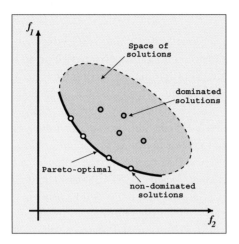

Fig. 5.9   The concept of Pareto-optimal with non-dominated solutions in the space of solutions.

If no further information about the objectives of the problem are given, the Pareto-optimal solutions are equally important. Therefore a decision making process is necessary to select an appropriate solution based on the most significant information for a given problem. In this context, the main goal is to find a set of solutions having a high diversity to provide as much information as possible about the solutions for the problem.

MOEAs involve a number of concepts and operators, such as dominance, niching, ranking, fitness sharing, external population and others [Deb (2001)]. The concepts of dominance and fitness ranking strategies applied to EA were initially proposed by Goldberg [Goldberg (1989)] and his studies provided the basis for modern MOEAs. One of the main ideas to define fitness values is to use the dominance rank strategy - the number of individuals by which an individual is dominated. Another approach, the dominance count, computes the number of individuals dominated by a certain individual to rank the individuals.

We investigated a number of multiobjective evolutionary optimization methods and applied two of the most up-to-date methods (SPEA2 and NSGA-II) to our range image registration problem. The target of these experiments was not to directly compare MOEAs, but to exploit their strength as an optimization tool to find precise alignments between views by using our robust fitness functions f and g (objective functions), as described on pages 50 and 89, respectively. By using MOEAs we can easily incorporate other objective functions, without the need of modifications to the algorithm's structure.

The SPEA2 [Zitzler *et al.* (2002)] and NSGA-II [Deb *et al.* (2002)] algorithms are recent improvements on the Strength Pareto Evolutionary Algorithm (SPEA) and the Non-dominated Sorting Genetic Algorithm (NSGA), respectively. These two methods have distinct approaches and recently, extensive comparative studies [Khare *et al.* (2003)], [Zitzler *et al.* (2002)] show that SPEA2 and NSGA-II have superior performance against their predecessors and other well-known methods for different classes of problems.

The SPEA was developed based on the main of advantages of many MOEAs proposed earlier. Basically, SPEA uses the dominance concept in the fitness assignment scheme and a clustering process to reduce the number of non-dominated solutions. The main objective of this approach is to preserve a uniform distribution of Pareto-optimal solutions using niching concepts [Deb (2001)]. To eliminate the potential weaknesses of its predecessor, the SPEA2 [Zitzler *et al.* (2002)] improved a revised fitness assignment strategy by using both dominance rank and count approaches and incorporates a nearest neighbor density estimation technique which allows a more precise searching process.

NSGA was one of the first MOEAs and was based on a Goldberg's suggestion of non-dominance [Goldberg (1989)]. The idea behind the non-dominated sorting procedure is that a ranking selection method is used to emphasize good solutions and a niching strategy keeps stable subpopulations of distinct good solutions. In its successor, the NSGA-II [Deb *et al.* (2002)], improvements to decrease the execution time and a density estimation and a crowding comparison operator were incorporated to guarantee a uniform distribution of good solutions along the Pareto-optimal front.

We conducted several experiments in registering different view pairs using both methods, SPEA2 and NSGA-II, and evaluated their final best solutions. The solutions found by NSGA-II presented slight better results than SPEA2. Figure 5.10 shows a result using the same view pair for 10 runs of each technique. Figure 5.11 highlights the correct registrations of Figure 5.10. The best result in terms of interpenetration for NSGA-II had SIM=69.8% and for SPEA2 had SIM=66.0%. For the same view pair the GH algorithm returned SIM=80.1 and the Robust GH had SIM=84.5%. Figure 5.12 shows a comparison of registration results for this example.

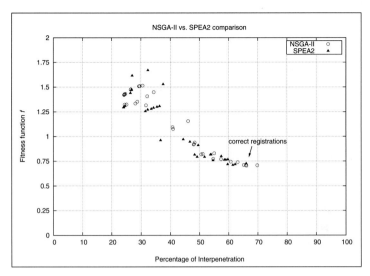

Fig. 5.10 Evaluation results of a view pair of object bird for 10 runs of each MOEA method.

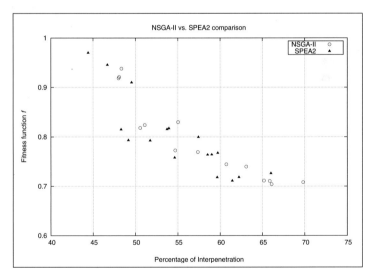

Fig. 5.11 Evaluation results of correct registrations regions as marked in Figure 5.10.

Both methods present a high diversity in the final solution set, but generally NSGA-II returned better solutions. Another observation is that SPEA2 is slower than NSGA-II, and in general both methods fail to provide precise alignments in terms of interpenetration because the methods exhibit the same difficulty in fine-tuning the solutions by GAs, addressed in Chapter 3.5.

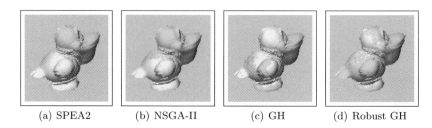

| (a) SPEA2 | (b) NSGA-II | (c) GH | (d) Robust GH |

Fig. 5.12   Registration results for a view pair of object bird.

The algorithms are implemented according to their description in the literature and these experiments yields promising results for range image registration using MOEAs. Recently, the Evolutionary Computation Group at ETH Zrich made available[2] an interesting platform for development of MOEA algorithms, implemented using a Petri nets architecture.

We use a standard GA as presented in Chapter 3.5 as the evolutionary procedure in the MOEAs without applying any hybrid combination, such as the hillclimbing heuristic (GH method). In comparison with our previous results, obtained by the GH, the MOEAs presented good registration results. However, we observe that the hillclimbing procedure in GH-based methods is more effective at achieving precise alignments. As future work we intend to explore in depth the use of MOEAs for range image registration.

The main advantage of MOEAs for range image registration is that one can introduce additional measures to guide the alignment process to make the registration more robust. As reported in Chapter , many range image registration methods use different image features in the registration process, for example surface curvatures [Chua and Jarvis (1996)] or edge maps [Sappa *et al.* (2001)]. We have begun to conduct some experiments using image features [Vieira *et al.* (2002), Bellon and Silva (2002)] to define correspondences between range views to aid the 3D modeling process. We intend to explore combinations of different image features and measures to define other objectives for MOEA for range registration purposes (see Chapter 5.4 for a detailed discussion of this issue).

[2]http://www.tik.ee.ethz.ch/pisa

5.4 Discussion

By combining both measures, MSE and SIM, we obtained a significant improvement in range image registration. Because the SIM is a more effective measure for precise alignment, we developed a robust registration method based on the GH technique, in which the SIM is used at the end of evolutionary process to refine the result. The results show a significant improvement in alignment quality. With this Robust GH approach we can guarantee precise registration and we will use this approach for multiview registration, in Chapter 5.4.

We explored the use of Multiobjective Evolutionary Algorithms (MOEAs) in range image registration problem, since we identified that it is necessary to combine measures to improve the registration results. Although MOEAs present good results, the solutions are not precise because the MOEAs experience the same difficulty in fine-tuning the solutions through the evolutionary process. This problem was addressed in Chapter 3.5. Furthermore, we know that MOEAs are promising solutions for many optimization problems and we intend to explore this research area in depth.

The main advantage of MOEAs is that one can easily introduce other objective functions to the problem without great modifications to the main implementation. By adding other objective functions, for example measures based on surface curvatures, one can obtain a more robust approach to range image registration.

Chapter 6

Multiview Range Image Registration

This chapter introduces a new approach to multiview range image registration based on our previous GA techniques. First, in Section 6.1 we describe how to obtain precise alignments in a common overlapping area among views. The idea is to guarantee precise alignment by using a set of overlapped views before the global registration stage. In Section 6.2 we present a global registration method using GAs to refine the registration between view pairs to provide a reliable global alignment for a subsequent 3D modeling stage. Section 6.3 presents experimental results in comparison with an other approach based on ICP. Finally, in Section 6.4 we present new ideas to eliminate inconsistent alignment regions by using the SIM. Regions on the surface of the object's views with no interpenetration are eliminated to provide a consistent alignment among views. We conclude the chapter with a discussion of results in Section 6.5.

6.1 Aligning common overlapping areas

In 3D modeling it is necessary to minimize the number of views to be aligned because data acquisition is expensive, and also to reduce error accumulation in the final model [Ikeuchi and Sato (2001)]. Since our GA-based techniques can deal with low-overlap views effectively, we apply the same idea to register multiple views, simultaneously.

Many approaches to multiview registration consider only the pairwise error between neighboring views in the global registration calculation [Blais and Levine (1995),Levoy *et al.* (2000),Huber and Hebert (2003)]. Yet it is typical for the image set to exhibit significant, common, overlapping regions in more than two neighboring views. This represents an important consideration in multiview registration.

Huber [Huber and Hebert (2003)] recently developed a multiview registration method to solve the unconstrained n-view problem. The method assumes no knowledge of initial pose, nor even of which views overlap. However, the problem of inaccurate alignment between some views is evident, owing to the local convergence of ICP in the first stage. Nevertheless, their experimental results show that for some objects the resulting 3D model preserves topology without significant distortion. They also point out that multiview surface matching is NP-complete. To obtain a good solution, a good pre-alignment is required for each combination of overlapping views before attempting global registration.

Based on these observations, we developed a new method for multiview registration using GAs. Our approach combines GH with the SIM to obtain a precise alignment of low-overlap views. The objective is to provide good alignment among more than two overlapping views before global registration to generate a precise 3D model. More precisely, we want to solve the following problem:

Given a set V of range views of an object having a common, overlapping area with respect to one fixed view, v_i, find the best transformation of each view v_j that precisely aligns it with v_i, with $v_i, v_j \in V$ and $v_i \neq v_j$.

We represent the possible solutions as a chromosome string using six genes for each view $v_j \in V$ representing three rotation parameters and three for translation, similar to the work in Chapter 3.5.

The fitness function is defined as:

$$h = \sum_{v_j \in V} f_{(v_j, v_i)} + e_{v_i} \tag{6.1}$$

where $f_{(v_j, v_i)}$ is the result of the cost function f (as defined in Chapter 3.5), with v_j as image A and v_i as image B. The registration error in the common overlap area is denoted by e_{v_i}. For this, we generalize the interpenetration operator C (defined in Eq. 3.1 in Chapter 2.5, page 22) of the SIM to find the set S of common interpenetrating points in v_i, with S defined as:

$$S_{v_i} = \bigcap_{v_j \in V} C_{(v_i, v_j)} \tag{6.2}$$

where $C_{(v_i, v_j)}$ is the set of interpenetration points in v_i with respect to v_j, with $v_i, v_j \in V$ and $v_i \neq v_j$. We then define e as:

$$e_{v_i} = \frac{\sum_{v_j \in V} \sum_{p \in S_{v_i}} k_{p_{(v_i, v_j)}}}{|S_{v_i}|(|V| - 1)} \tag{6.3}$$

where $k_{p_{(v_i, v_j)}}$ is the squared distance between the point $p \in S$ and its corresponding point in v_j, with $v_i, v_j \in V$ and $v_i \neq v_j$. We also compute the fraction of common overlap points in v_i (similar to the SIM equation) as:

$$O_{v_i} = \frac{|S_{v_i}|}{|v_i|} \tag{6.4}$$

where $|S_{v_i}|$ and $|v_i|$ are the numbers of points in S_{v_i} and in v_i, respectively.

The objective in using h (Equation 6.1) is to find the best combination of the alignments for each view that minimizes the sum of their f values while preserving a minimal error within the common overlapping area, as given by e.

The preliminary experiments were performed using the OSU range image database. From this database, we used objects comprising free-form surfaces, imaged in 18 views acquired at 20 degree intervals using a computer-controlled turntable and the Minolta Vivid 700 scanner. From the set of views of each object we observed that even views taken 80 degrees apart have some common, overlapping area between them.

The multiview registration tests were performed using sets of three low-overlap views of each object, taken at 40 degree intervals, to demonstrate the effectiveness of this approach. The method can be readily extended to more than three views, but we found no instance of a common area among four low-overlap views (with 40 degree spacing) in the database.

In these experiments, the chromosome string is defined by 12 genes for two views - six each representing three rotation parameters and three for translation. Then, the objective of the evolutionary process is to find the transformation of the two views together, v_1 and v_2, that best aligns them with the third view, v_3, to generate an accurate registration for this part of the object. In this process we also consider the registration error in the common overlap of v_1 and v_2, as defined in Eq. 6.3.

We compared our multiview registration approach to pairwise registration strategies using ICP and GH methods. In the pairwise registration, the views are registered sequentially, v_1 to v_3 and v_2 to v_3. After that, we combined both pairwise alignments and computed the SIM and O_{v_3} to compare with the new technique.

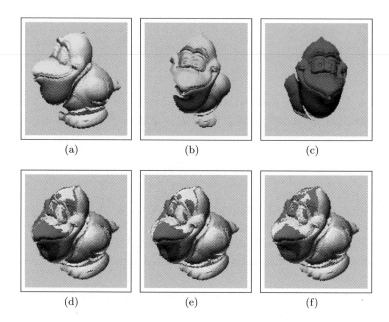

(a)   (b)   (c)

(d)   (e)   (f)

Fig. 6.1   Multiview registration results for different views of the same object: (a) view 340 degrees, v_1; (b) view 20 degrees, v_3; (c) view 60 degrees, v_2; (d) result of pairwise registration using GH; (e) result of pairwise registration using ICP; and (f) result of multiview registration.

Figure 6.1 shows an example result from the multiview formulation, where views v_1 and v_2 represent the most separated views, to be aligned with the middle view, v_3.   The obtained results are: Figure 6.1(d) $SIM_{v_1,v_3} = 34.70\%$, $SIM_{v_2,v_3} = 33.42\%$, $O_{v_3} = 11.08\%$ and $e_{v_3} = 0.19$; Figure 6.1(e) $SIM_{v_1,v_3} = 25.42\%$, $SIM_{v_2,v_3} = 31.02\%$, $O_{v_3} = 7.19\%$ and $e_{v_3} = 0.28$; Figure 6.1(f) $SIM_{v_1,v_3} = 31.74\%$, $SIM_{v_2,v_3} = 32.76\%$, $O_{v_3} = 14.42\%$ and $e_{v_3} = 0.10$.

These results show that the multiview approach distributes the error between the alignments while preserving a good SIM between views. As can be seen, our approach generates superior alignments in the common overlap area, given by O_{v_3}.

The results over different objects and combinations of views show an improvement, with respect to the common overlap area, of about 20% compared to pairwise GH and about 40% compared to pairwise ICP. Figure 6.2 shows different views of the multiview registration shown in Figure 6.1(f) and the distinct alignments between each pair of views.

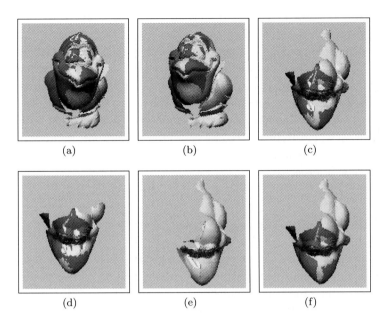

(a) (b) (c)

(d) (e) (f)

Fig. 6.2   Different views (a)-(c) of the registration results obtained by the multiview approach in Figure 6.1(f) and each combination of alignments: (d) views v_2 and v_3; (e) v_1 and v_2 and (f) views v_1 and v_3.

In the multiview experiments, we first tried the same GA parameter settings given in Chapter 3.5. However, it was necessary to increase the number of generations and population size to ensure good convergence. This is not surprising because the number of search space dimensions has doubled from six to 12. Multiview (3-view) registration using 300 generations, with $pop = 500$ and each image having approximately 10000 3D points, takes approximately 80 minutes on a Pentium 4 - 1.7 GHz processor. The computational time of the GAs can be significantly reduced if the process is performed in parallel on a cluster of machines [Robertson and Fisher (2002)] and if a sampling process is applied on each view, as presented in Chapter 3.5.

As the experimental results illustrate, our method provides robust performance in finding correct registrations with large interpenetration in the area common to the three views. This is crucial for the construction of 3D models from multiple views, minimizing error accumulation in the final model. Also, our method can deal with low-overlap views, which can be critical for 3D modeling applications, because the number of views to be acquired and aligned (often at significant cost and/or time) can be significantly reduced.

Also, as presented in Chapter 4.10, one can use the Robust GH approach instead of GH to improve the alignment between view pairs and make the multiview process even more robust. In fact, the multiview approach distributes the error among all alignments much as the Robust GH distributes the error over the alignment between two views. By combining both ideas, the multiview and Robust GH, one can obtain significant improvements in terms of global alignment. In Section 6.2 we discuss this issue in a global registration approach.

6.2 Global multiview registration

The objective of the global multiview registration process is to provide good alignment between overlapping views as well as precise positions for all views of the object in a common coordinate system. This process is the key to subsequent 3D modeling stage, mainly in the fusion stage, in which one must preserve as much detail as possible. To support this, it is essential to use a robust registration method that can precisely align two or more views while preserving object geometry.

We designed a global multiview registration method in three stages: 1) initial alignments of view pairs using GH with the MSE-based fitness function f (minimization problem); 2) refinement of the registration results of stage 1 using GH with the SIM-based fitness function g (maximization problem) to obtain precise alignments; 3) global registration based on a multiview GH approach, with a compound fitness function based on the SIM to generate the final alignment among all views, as presented in Section 6.1. We note that stages 1 and 2 can be merged into a single process using the Robust GH of Chapter 4.10. Here, we elected to use two stages to clarify the improvement offered by each.

In a typical multiview registration process the preliminary stage identifies the relationships between views and delineates overlapping areas. Generally, the correspondences between views are defined during on-the-fly data acquisition [Ikeuchi and Sato (2001)] or by posterior visual analysis with human supervision. Recently, an alternative approach [Huber and Hebert (2003)] was used to try to find the best set of relationships by computing all possible alignments between view pairs generating a complete graph, and searching this graph for the minimal spanning tree. This "brute force" approach is based on ICP registration; consequently, local inconsistencies may occur because ICP has local convergence problems.

In this direction, we investigated the use of data mining strategies to find view correspondences through high level feature analysis [Vieira *et al.* (2002)]. We have developed a range image mining tool to help with this problem of corresponding view identification. With this, one can obtain good hypotheses of overlapping views automatically on which to perform global multiview registration.

Because the objects from the OSU range image database we are using were acquired with a turntable, the identification of corresponding views is given by their number in the database. To perform multiview registration we first select a set V of n consecutive low-overlap views. From the set of 18 views of each object we selected 9 consecutive views, taken at 40 degree intervals. For these objects the relationship between consecutive views is given by the circular graph in Figure 6.3(a). However, our global multiview registration method can be extended to accept other graph configurations as input. We summarize the process as follows.

Stage 0: Create the graph of view relationships. In this experiment we generate a circular graph (see Figure 6.3(a)) by using consecutive views, acquired using a turntable and separated by 40 degrees.

Stage 1: Performed registration using GH with f as fitness function (see Eq. 4.4, page 50) for each successive view pair, given by the graph of Figure 6.3(a), in the clockwise direction. The alignment between v_n and v_1, with n the number of views in V, is indirectly obtained when the views are positioned in a common coordinate system. We use the same GA parameter settings given in Chapter 3.5.

Stage 2: Since each pair of views is now aligned, we refine these alignments by performing GH using g as the fitness function (SIM-based function of Chapter 4.10) in a reduced search space. In the experiments we restricted the range of rotations and translations to 10% of the range values used in Stage 1. After that, we position the aligned views in a common coordinate system by fixing an aligned pair, *e.g.* (v_{n-1}, v_n), and applying transformations to the other view pairs sequentially in a counterclockwise direction from the view pair (v_{n-1}, v_n) to (v_1, v_2). These transformations are easily obtained because each neighboring pair has a view in common, and consequently the corresponding points between views are known exactly. We use a unit quaternion [Besl and McKay (1992)] from the point correspondences to find the rotation matrices and translation vectors.

Stage 3: In the last stage, a global alignment is obtained by using GH with the chromosome string defined by $6 \times (n-1)$ genes for $n-1$ views $(v_1, v_2, ..., v_{n-1})$; six each representing three rotation parameters and three for translation. Then, the objective of the evolutionary process is to find the transformation of $n-1$ views together that best aligns them with the fixed view v_n to generate an accurate global registration for the object. Since we can expect the previous stages o supply precise pairwise alignments, one can use a SIM-based function alone to generate the final global registration. We compute the SIM for both directions of alignment (clockwise and counterclockwise) and in the common overlap for both neighbors of each view, *e.g.* views v_2 and v_4 are the neighboring views of v_3. Because even views taken 80 degrees apart have some common, overlapping area between them, we also considered the SIM within these areas in stage 3 by using a compound fitness function u, similar to h as given in Section 6.1.

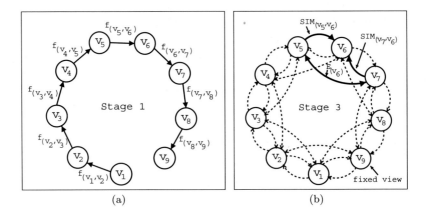

Fig. 6.3   Illustration of the multiview registration stages: (a) registrations computed in stage 1 (in stage 2, the same configuration is applied but using the SIM-based fitness function g, instead of f); (b) computed measures for each view in stage 3 to generate the global registration from a fixed view.

Figure 6.3(b) shows the measures computed in stage 3. Obviously, this process is very time consuming, but since the views are already aligned we can reduce the search space to small rotations and translations. We can also reduce the number of points by sampling to increase speed. Finally, we can apply the method using a parallel architecture, which has shown great promise lately. Nevertheless, to our knowledge, this approach to multiview range image registration using GAs has never been done before.

The compound fitness function u used in Stage 3 is defined as:

$$u = \sum_{v_i \in V} \left(SIM_{(v_{i-1}, v_i)} + SIM_{(v_{i+1}, v_i)} + E_{(v_i)} \right) \qquad (6.5)$$

where v_{i-1} and v_{i+1} are the neighboring views of v_i with $v_i, v_{i-1}, v_{i+1} \in V$. The SIM in the common overlapping area of the neighboring views of a given view is computed by $E_{(v_i)}$, similar to Section 6.1. For this, we compute the set C of interpenetrating points in v_i with respect to its neighbors. We define $E_{(v_i)}$ as:

$$E_{(v_i)} = \frac{|C_{(v_i, v_{i-1})} \cap C_{(v_i, v_{i+1})}|}{|v_i|} \qquad (6.6)$$

where v_{i-1} and v_{i+1} are the neighbors of v_i with $v_i, v_{i-1}, v_{i+1} \in V$.

Using function u we obtain a better distribution of interpenetration for each aligned view pair, as presented in Section 6.3. We observed that the configuration of the corresponding points underwent no significant changes during the convergence process because after stages 1 and 2 the views are quite precisely aligned. To reduce the computational time needed to find the corresponding points from one view to another in the SIM computation, we can start the search from the last position of each closest point of the last generation in the GH, as proposed in [Greenspan and Godin (2001)]. This can be safely applied because the search space in stage 3 is confined within small ranges and the alignment between views undergoes no significant modifications during the process.

6.3 Experimental results

We compared the multiview registration approach against ICP and GH pairwise registration strategies [Silva *et al.* (2003a), Silva *et al.* (2003b)]. In pairwise registration, the views are registered sequentially, as described for stage 1 of our method (see Section 6.2), and positioned in a common coordinate system. After that, we computed the SIM and the MSE of each aligned view pair to analyze the results. Figures 6.4 and 6.5 show an example of registrations obtained for each approach for visual comparison. The final alignment produced by ICP pairwise registration reveals grossly erroneous alignments, as shown in Figures 6.4(d) and 6.5(d) (Note the tail of the object "bird" is erroneously aligned).

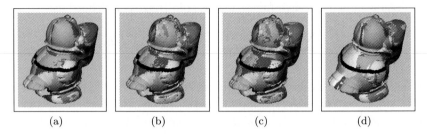

Fig. 6.4 Comparison of global alignments: (a) after stage 1 of our multiview method; (b) after stage 2 of our multiview method; (c) final global registration of our multiview approach; (d) pairwise ICP approach.

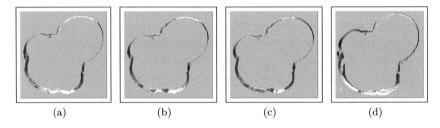

Fig. 6.5 Comparison results of global alignments: (a)-(d) cross sections (black line) of the registrations in Figure 6.4, respectively.

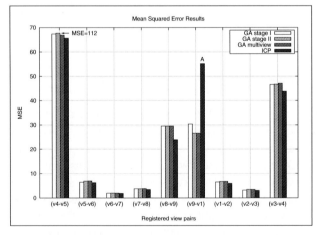

Fig. 6.6 MSE comparison for each aligned view pairs of the object in Figure 6.4. To provide a better plot visualization, MSE values of the alignment (v_4-v_5) are reduced by 40 units; the real values are around 112.

Figures 6.6 and 6.7 plot the results of MSE and SIM for each aligned view pair, respectively. These results show that our multiview approach, while achieving typical MSE results very near those of ICP, better distributes the error among the alignments while preserving a good SIM between views. The situation A in Figure 6.6 (ICP result for v_9-v_1) shows that ICP fails in this indirect alignment because the accumulated error of aligned views is high.

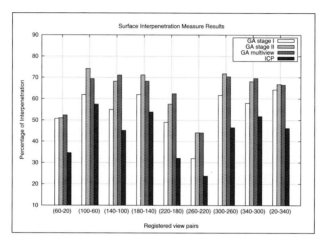

Fig. 6.7   Computed SIM for each aligned view pairs of the object in Figure 6.4.

We also compared the MSE and SIM averages for each technique, as presented in Table 6.1. In this comparison we recomputed the MSE and SIM of each view pair in the clockwise direction, as shown in Figure 6.3(a), at the end of the multiview method and ICP pairwise approaches. The results considering only the aligned view pairs (see Figure 6.3(a)), without including the indirect alignment (v_9, v_1), show that ICP had the lowest MSE average. However, when the indirect alignment is accounted for, the ICP average MSE is far worse because of the significant accumulation of error in the ICP pairwise alignments. GH exhibits no significant accumulation of error at the end of each stage (see MSE average results in the Table 6.1). In stage 2, using the SIM as the fitness function, we obtained precise alignments with high SIM values, while preserving a low MSE. Finally, the multiview approach (stage 3) shows good SIM and global redistribution of MSE among all the alignments (including v_9, v_1) and presents both the highest SIM and the lowest MSE averages overall.

Table 6.1   MSE and SIM averages of the experimental tests. The rows represent the average of aligned view pairs with and without the indirect alignment (v_9, v_1), respectively.

Aligned view	GH stage 1		GH stage 2		Multiview		ICP	
pairs	MSE	SIM%	MSE	SIM%	MSE	SIM%	MSE	SIM%
$without(v_9, v_1)$	26.30	57.81	26.47	66.10	26.44	66.24	24.87	45.94
$with(v_9, v_1)$	26.75	54.94	26.49	63.66	26.46	63.78	28.24	43.47

The results over different objects and combinations of views show an improvement in the SIM, with respect to global alignment, of about 10% compared to GH (at the end of stage 1) and 30% compared to pairwise ICP. We also observed that at the end of stage 2, the global alignment is reasonable due to the robust and effective SIM measure. In the multiview experiments (stage 3), we first tried the same GH parameter settings given in stage 2 of our multiview method. However, it was necessary to increase the number of generations to 500 to ensure good convergence. This is not surprising because the number of search space dimensions has increased dramatically, from 6 to 48.

Multiview registration using 500 generations takes approximately 8 hours on a 1.7 GHz Pentium 4 processor. Of course, the computational time of the GAs can be significantly reduced if the process is performed in parallel using a cluster of machines [Robertson and Fisher (2002)]. Also, this time can be reduced if we apply sampling before the registration to reduce the number of 3D points in each view.

Although time consuming, we observed that our approach is efficient in terms of obtaining precise alignments. We observed that even after stage 2 the views are correctly positioned, giving a reliable registration between all views. Since registration between view pairs is critical for effective multiview registration, the Robust GH is the most powerful method for this purpose.

6.4   Alignment consistency

After all views are precisely aligned, views can be fused to generate the 3D model. This process, also known as surface reconstruction, is usually accomplished by a volumetric approach [Curless and Levoy (1996)], in which the data from multiple views are combined into a single and compact volumetric representation of the object.

One of the main problems in surface reconstruction is the need to eliminate the redundancy of overlaps between view pairs. Generally, a weighted average is performed for nearby points that are considered to be from the same region. However, it is essential to have precise registrations, or alignment consistency, to avoid 3D model distortion [Ikeuchi and Sato (2001)].

Considering that we usually have many regions with a common overlapping area, if the views are not sufficiently close, the surface reconstruction result may generate overly smooth surfaces or even small distortions in the 3D model. Thus, the registration results, even for pair of views, must be robust to generate precise alignments. The Robust GH enjoys a great advantage in this process, because we use the SIM to drive the final refinement and the results contain large interpenetrating surfaces. Consequently, in the surface reconstruction stage one can accept small errors between views and still obtain precise 3D models.

Motivated by this observation, we performed some experiments using the SIM as a measure of alignment consistency for subsequent surface reconstruction. After the global multiview registration is complete we can locate in each view those points having no interpenetration with neighboring views. Thus, we can discard all these points to supply consistent overlapping regions in the global registration. Our experiments have shown that noise regions present in many views of the objects in the OSU range image database can be eliminated through this simple rule using the SIM. Eventually, some gaps may appear in the "noise free" surface of the object, where the views are aligned but have parallel regions with no interpenetration (this effect can be seen in some experiments in Chapter 2.5).

Figure 6.8 shows the result of eliminating non-interpenetrating points of the global alignment shown in Figure 6.4 in Section 6.3. As can be seen, some gaps appear in the object surface, indicating that in these regions it is necessary to add other overlapping views to provide a more accurate surface covering. Despite the small gaps, the alignment is very precise and reveals good overall interpenetration. Figure 6.9 shows cross sections (black line) of the registrations in Figure 6.8 illustrating that many inconsistent regions (noise regions) were eliminated. We intend to investigate the use of the SIM in a surface reconstruction method for precise 3D model generation in the near future.

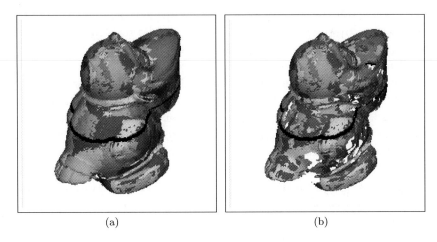

Fig. 6.8   Comparison results of global alignments: (a) the same global registration of Figure 6.4 and (b) the result by eliminating non-interpenetrating points.

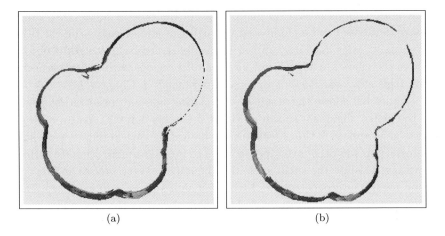

Fig. 6.9   Comparison results of global alignments: (a) and (b) are cross sections (black line) of the registrations in Figures 6.8(a) and 6.8(b), respectively.

6.5   Discussion

We developed a novel robust approach for the precise registration of multiple range images. The method is based on the GH implementation and the

Surface Interpenetration Measure (SIM) from earlier in this book. As the experimental results illustrate, our method provides excellent, robust performance in finding correct registrations with large interpenetrating areas. Also, our method deals effectively with low-overlap views, which can be critical for many applications, because the number of views to be acquired (often at significant cost and/or time) and aligned can be significantly reduced. For archaeology and related domains, speed is (usually) less important than precision and robustness; our approach would be the method of choice in such cases. As future work, we wish to explore a parallel version to accelerate the method.

One important result we observed was that, following stage 2 of multiview registration, the views are precisely aligned, well-positioned in a common coordinate system. Thus, the Robust GH approach is highly effective for the initial stages of a multiview range image registration system.

We also addressed the use of the SIM as a measure of surface consistency to provide precise regions of the global alignment for subsequent surface reconstruction. The results are very promising and we intend to explore this idea in the future.

Chapter 7

Closing Comments

We conclude this book with an overview of the work followed by a discussion of our main contributions and directions for future work in Section 7.1 and 7.2, respectively.

In this book, we have identified the major problems in automatically obtaining precise alignments between range images for 3D model construction. We approached these problems by first defining a new evaluation measure, the Surface Interpenetration Measure (SIM), to quantify the registration quality and to guide the alignment process. We explored the use of stochastic methods, in particular, Genetic Algorithms (GAs), for the range image registration problem, and developed a robust approach by combining GAs with the SIM to overcome the drawbacks of other methods. Our robust approach yielded superior solutions compared with other methods and was successfully applied to low-overlap views that may include substantial noise. We also applied our GA-based registration methods to the multiview registration problem to provide a precise global positioning of multiple views, since accurate registration is essential to generate reliable 3D models, avoiding model distortions and preserving as much detail as possible.

7.1 Contributions

In this book we can identify seven primary contributions:

- The Surface Interpenetration Measure (SIM) - We proposed a new concept to precisely measure the alignment of range images by computing the interpenetration between surfaces. The main contribution is that the SIM has the ability to better distribute the alignment error over the overlapping areas to provide precise registration. Also, we confirmed that the SIM can efficiently guide the registration process to generate more accurate solutions than MSE-based measures.

- Stochastic methods for range image registration - We explored in depth several aspects of stochastic methods, in particular Genetic Algorithms, for range image registration. We identified the main strengths and weaknesses of these methods and proposed a robust approach to overcome the need for pre-alignments and to avoid the local convergence issues of ICP-based methods, which are most popular to date.

- Enhanced GAs - We proposed several improvements to enhance the GA-based techniques to achieve more precise alignment for range image registration. We explored the combination with Simulated Annealing (SA) procedures and local search heuristics, such as hillclimbing, to simulate "shaking" the surface to better adjust the result. Thus, one can obtain precise alignments in terms of MSE or SIM measures.

- Robust range image registration - We combined our GA-based approach with the SIM to generate an effective and robust technique for range image registration. The results show that our robust approach outperformed other techniques, delivering superior alignments.

- Range image registration as a multiobjective problem - We identified that to obtain precise registrations it is necessary to combine different measures to generate a more robust technique. We defined range image registration as a multiobjective problem and tested the most up-to-date multiobjective evolutionary algorithms to solve it. These experiments gave us promising ideas to improve registration by adding other objectives derived from image features.

- Multiview registration using GAs - We proposed a novel approach to multiview range image registration by combining the robust GA approach with the SIM. To our knowledge the application of GAs for multiview range image registration has never been done before.

- SIM for alignment consistency checking - We explored the use of the SIM as a measure for alignment consistency by eliminating non-interpenetrating points after the global multiview registration. The results show we can provide reliable alignment regions for subsequent surface reconstruction to generate precise 3D models.

Although our approach based on GAs is clearly more robust than ICP-based approaches, works for low-overlap, works under noisy conditions, and needs no pre-alignment, it must also be acknowledged that stochastic search techniques (including GAs) can be slow. In those domains for which speed is at a premium (or computational resources are limited) and the other issues are less significant, ICP may well be the preferred solution. For model-building, archaeology, and related domains, speed is (usually) less important than precision and robustness; our approach would be the method of choice in such cases. However, we already proposed the use of sampling methods to reduce the number of points to be aligned and parallel processing to speed up the GAs [Man *et al.* (1996)]. Also, the problem of parameter setting for GAs can be solved using parameter free approaches, as recently proposed [Sawai and Adachi (1999)].

For the SIM, our implementation is restricted to range images, in which a regular grid exists. We intend to extend this measure to 3D point clouds (with no regular grids, as supplied by some scanners) by adding a nearest neighbor search, limited by a threshold, instead of using a square window over which to compute the interpenetrating points. This can lead to more generic applications for the SIM.

7.2 Future work

We have several ideas to extend our work and promising applications to pursue in the near future. We can summarize most of them as follows:

- Parallel processing - We intend to developed a parallel version for our GA-based methods to speed up the range image registration process.
- Parameter free - We will investigate the parameter free approaches for GAs [Sawai and Adachi (1999)] to make our methods automatic and more generic, suitable for a variety of applications.
- Generic SIM - We intend to extend the SIM to deal with 3D point clouds in addition to range grids because there are many archaeological databases based on the 3D point cloud representation.
- Surface reconstruction - Since we have a robust multiview range image registration method, we intend to develop surface reconstruction methods based our work to generate precise 3D models from range images.
- Integration in the CBIRS3D - We intend to make our methods available to the content-based image retrieval system of 3D images and models (CBIRS3D) under development in the IMAGO group at Universidade Federal do Paran. The idea is to integrate the registration methods in the system to guide both reconstruction and visualization processes.

Appendix

Experimental Results

In this appendix we provide the registration results from the OSU range image database (sampl.eng.ohio-state.edu). As presented in Chapter 2.5, we used 496 view pairs of 4 objects (bird, duck, frog, teletubby), totaling 124 alignments for each.

Each object from the database has 18 views acquired using a turntable at 20 degree spacing and we combined views separated by 20 and 40 degrees, which gives a significant overlapping area between views. From this set of 496 view pairs, the ICP-based approaches returned 166 good alignments and 330 failed alignments. Because no pre-alignment was done the point-to-point correspondence search returned better results than did point-to-plane.

We present all the registrations obtained by the ICP-based approaches to provide a visual analysis. We also include the results obtained by the GH approach, as described in Chapter 3.5, to provide a visual comparison with the ICP results (for good alignments). In addition, we present all registration results obtained from view pairs of the object "bird" to illustrate the improvements obtained with GH as opposed to the erroneous alignments of ICP-based approaches.

The views of the registration results were rendered in different colors (green and yellow) using a triangulation method [Guibas and Stolfi (1985)]. The name of each registration figure is based on its acquisition angle from the turntable and the direction of the registration. For example, a sub-figure of the object "bird" named 20-60, shows view 20, image A (green), aligned with view 60, image B (yellow).

Figures A.1-A.10 present the results using point-to-point ICP-based registration and Figures A.13-A.23 present the results using point-to-plane ICP-based registration. To provide a visual comparison for the correct alignments obtained by ICP, Figures A.26-A.32 present the results using the GH method. To illustrate the efficiency of GH we include the rest of the registered view pairs of the object "bird", in which the ICP fails (see Figure A.36). Finally, Figs A.39-A.45 present the results of the Robust GH for comparison with the correct alignments of ICP and GH.

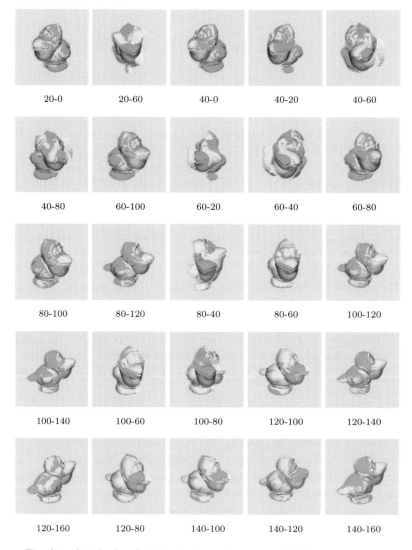

20-0	20-60	40-0	40-20	40-60
40-80	60-100	60-20	60-40	60-80
80-100	80-120	80-40	80-60	100-120
100-140	100-60	100-80	120-100	120-140
120-160	120-80	140-100	140-120	140-160

Fig. A.1   Results for object bird using point-to-point ICP-based approach.

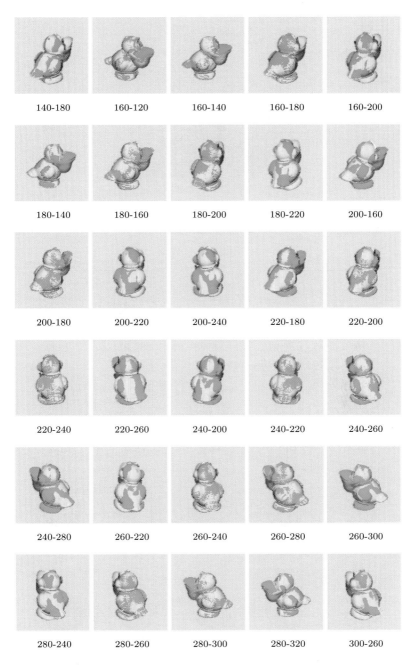

140-180   160-120   160-140   160-180   160-200

180-140   180-160   180-200   180-220   200-160

200-180   200-220   200-240   220-180   220-200

220-240   220-260   240-200   240-220   240-260

240-280   260-220   260-240   260-280   260-300

280-240   280-260   280-300   280-320   300-260

Fig. A.2   (*Continued*)

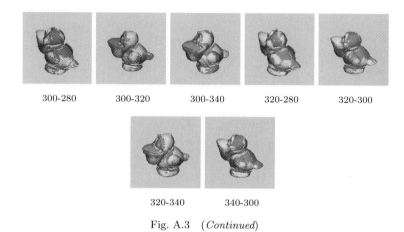

300-280   300-320   300-340   320-280   320-300

320-340   340-300

Fig. A.3   (*Continued*)

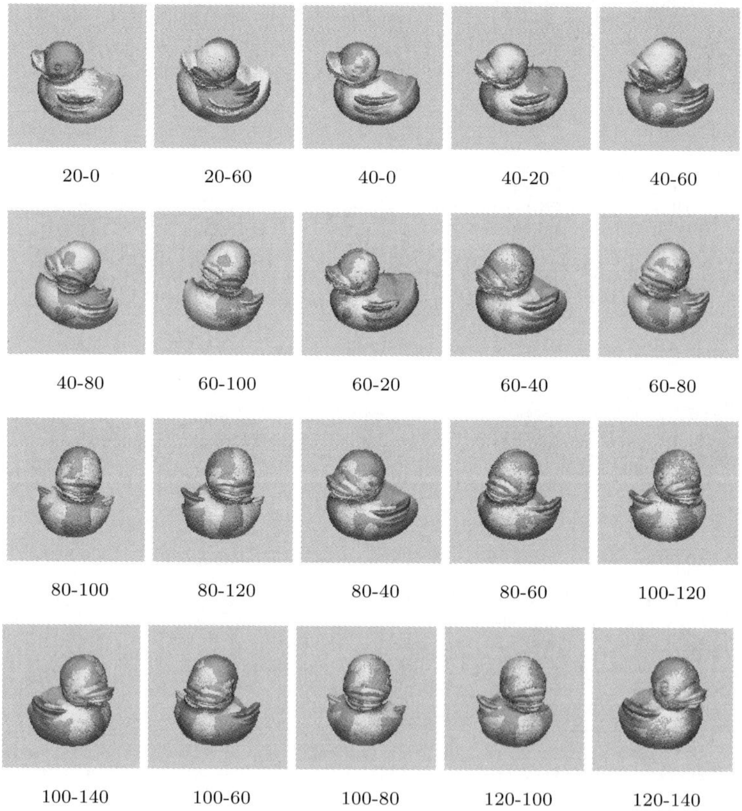

20-0   20-60   40-0   40-20   40-60

40-80   60-100   60-20   60-40   60-80

80-100   80-120   80-40   80-60   100-120

100-140   100-60   100-80   120-100   120-140

Fig. A.4   Results for object duck using point-to-point ICP-based approach.

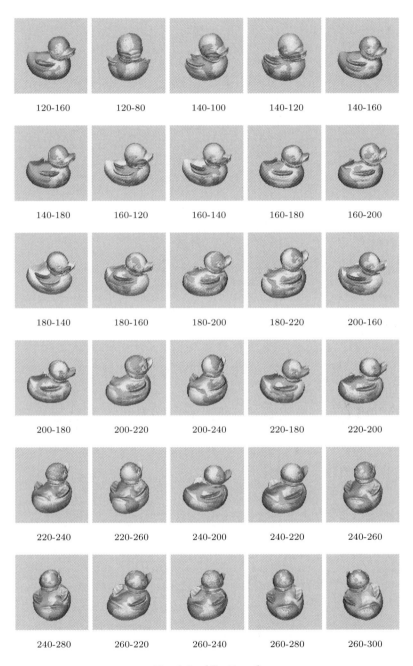

Fig. A.5 (*Continued*)

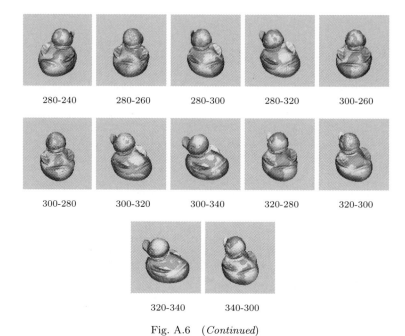

280-240   280-260   280-300   280-320   300-260

300-280   300-320   300-340   320-280   320-300

320-340   340-300

Fig. A.6   (*Continued*)

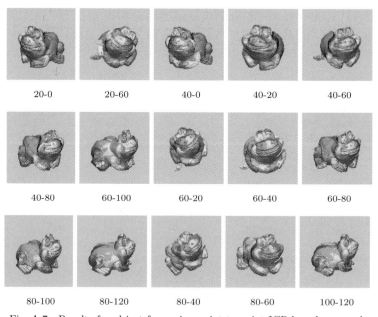

20-0   20-60   40-0   40-20   40-60

40-80   60-100   60-20   60-40   60-80

80-100   80-120   80-40   80-60   100-120

Fig. A.7   Results for object frog using point-to-point ICP-based approach.

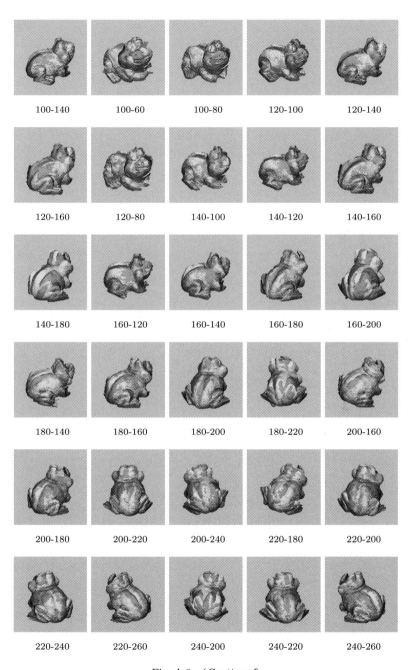

Fig. A.8 (*Continued*)

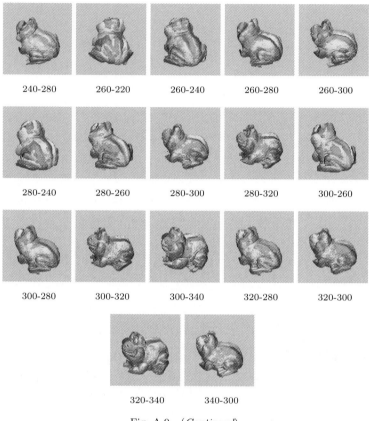

| 240-280 | 260-220 | 260-240 | 260-280 | 260-300 |

| 280-240 | 280-260 | 280-300 | 280-320 | 300-260 |

| 300-280 | 300-320 | 300-340 | 320-280 | 320-300 |

| 320-340 | 340-300 |

Fig. A.9   (*Continued*)

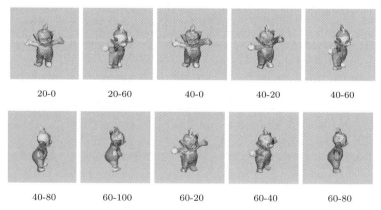

| 20-0 | 20-60 | 40-0 | 40-20 | 40-60 |

| 40-80 | 60-100 | 60-20 | 60-40 | 60-80 |

Fig. A.10   Results for object teletubby using point-to-point ICP-based approach.

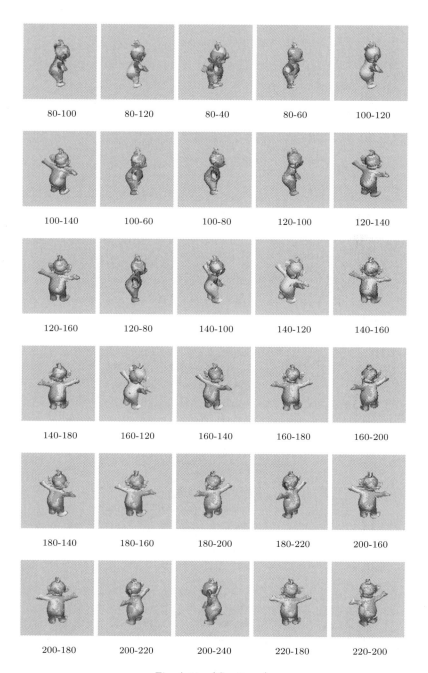

Fig. A.11 (*Continued*)

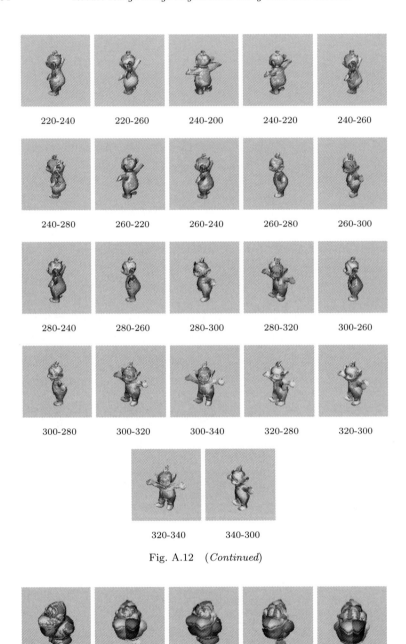

220-240   220-260   240-200   240-220   240-260

240-280   260-220   260-240   260-280   260-300

280-240   280-260   280-300   280-320   300-260

300-280   300-320   300-340   320-280   320-300

320-340   340-300

Fig. A.12   (*Continued*)

20-0   20-60   40-0   40-20   40-60

Fig. A.13   Results for object bird using point-to-plane ICP-based approach.

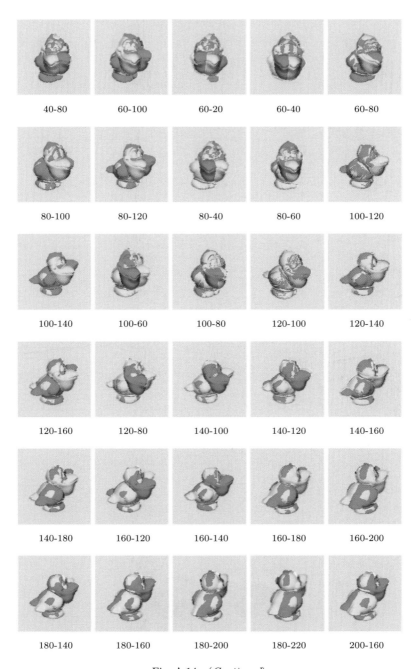

Fig. A.14   (*Continued*)

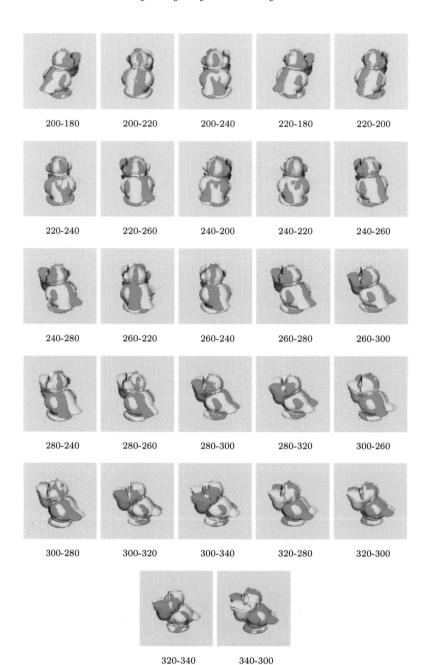

200-180   200-220   200-240   220-180   220-200

220-240   220-260   240-200   240-220   240-260

240-280   260-220   260-240   260-280   260-300

280-240   280-260   280-300   280-320   300-260

300-280   300-320   300-340   320-280   320-300

320-340   340-300

Fig. A.15   (*Continued*)

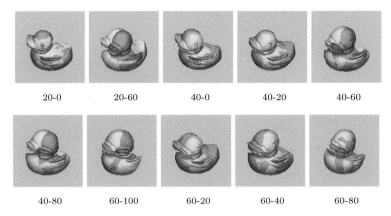

20-0 20-60 40-0 40-20 40-60

40-80 60-100 60-20 60-40 60-80

Fig. A.16   Results for object duck using point-to-plane ICP-based approach.

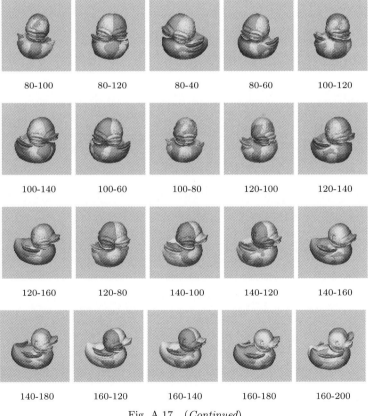

80-100 80-120 80-40 80-60 100-120

100-140 100-60 100-80 120-100 120-140

120-160 120-80 140-100 140-120 140-160

140-180 160-120 160-140 160-180 160-200

Fig. A.17   (*Continued*)

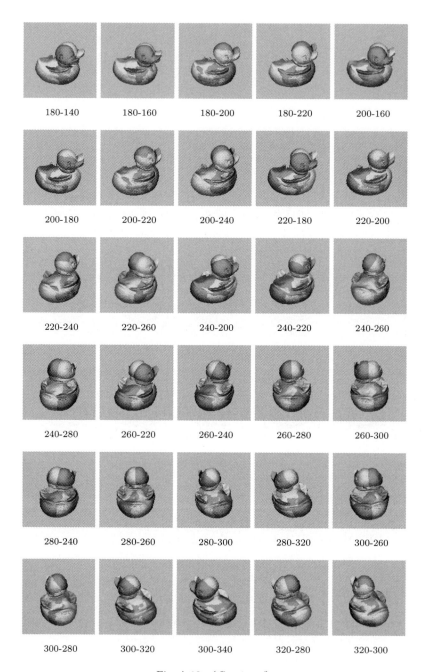

Fig. A.18   (*Continued*)

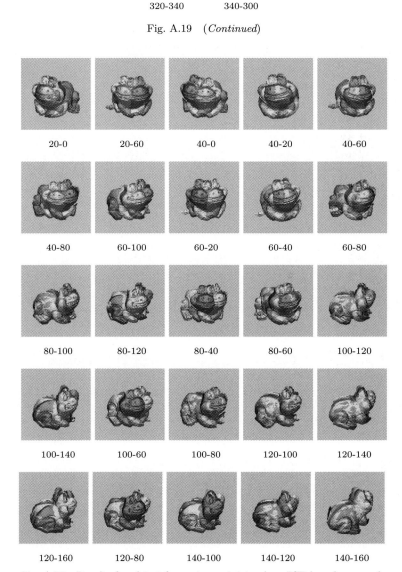

320-340   340-300

Fig. A.19   (*Continued*)

20-0   20-60   40-0   40-20   40-60

40-80   60-100   60-20   60-40   60-80

80-100   80-120   80-40   80-60   100-120

100-140   100-60   100-80   120-100   120-140

120-160   120-80   140-100   140-120   140-160

Fig. A.20   Results for object frog using point-to-plane ICP-based approach.

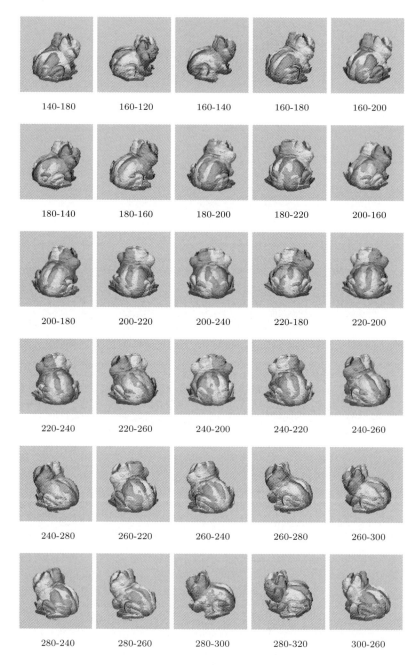

Fig. A.21 (*Continued*)

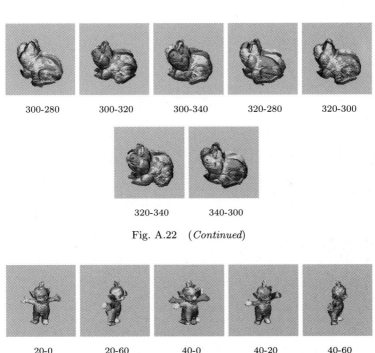

300-280   300-320   300-340   320-280   320-300

320-340   340-300

Fig. A.22   (*Continued*)

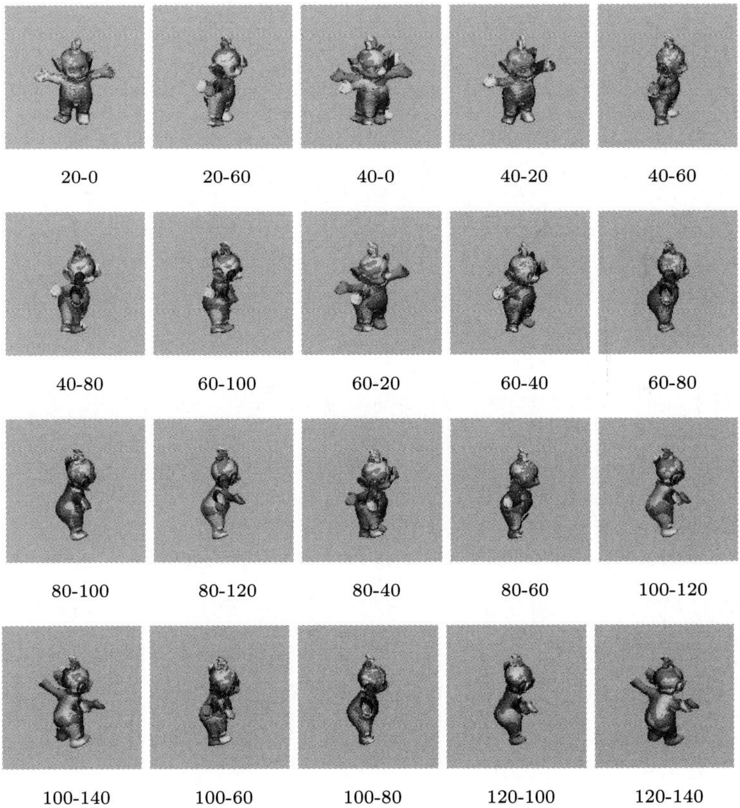

20-0   20-60   40-0   40-20   40-60

40-80   60-100   60-20   60-40   60-80

80-100   80-120   80-40   80-60   100-120

100-140   100-60   100-80   120-100   120-140

Fig. A.23   Results for object teletubby using point-to-plane ICP-based approach.

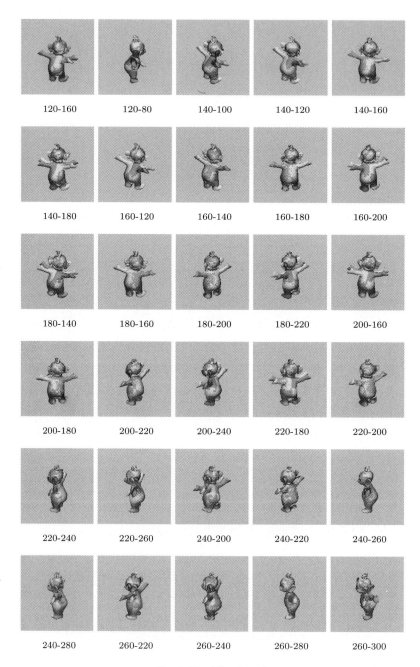

Fig. A.24 (*Continued*)

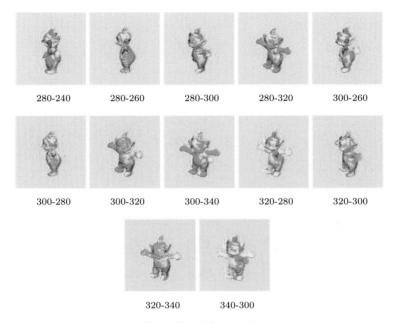

280-240   280-260   280-300   280-320   300-260

300-280   300-320   300-340   320-280   320-300

320-340   340-300

Fig. A.25   (*Continued*)

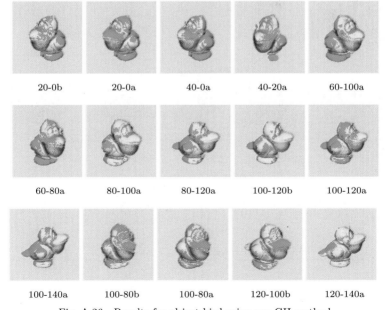

20-0b   20-0a   40-0a   40-20a   60-100a

60-80a   80-100a   80-120a   100-120b   100-120a

100-140a   100-80b   100-80a   120-100b   120-140a

Fig. A.26   Results for object bird using our GH method.

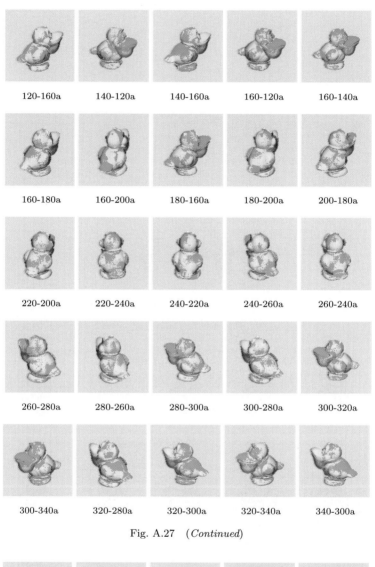

120-160a   140-120a   140-160a   160-120a   160-140a

160-180a   160-200a   180-160a   180-200a   200-180a

220-200a   220-240a   240-220a   240-260a   260-240a

260-280a   280-260a   280-300a   300-280a   300-320a

300-340a   320-280a   320-300a   320-340a   340-300a

Fig. A.27   (*Continued*)

20-0a   60-40a   80-60a   100-120a   120-140a

Fig. A.28   Results for object duck using our GH method.

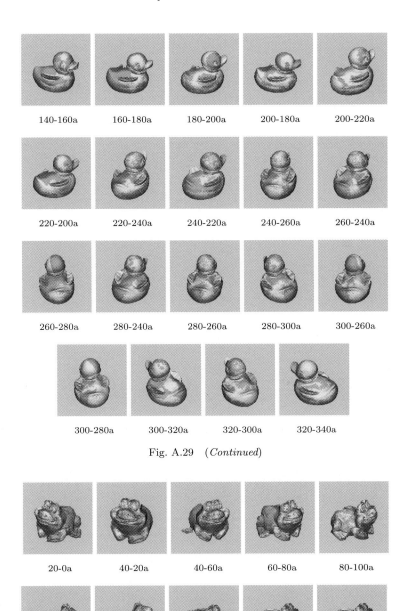

140-160a   160-180a   180-200a   200-180a   200-220a

220-200a   220-240a   240-220a   240-260a   260-240a

260-280a   280-240a   280-260a   280-300a   300-260a

300-280a   300-320a   320-300a   320-340a

Fig. A.29   (*Continued*)

20-0a   40-20a   40-60a   60-80a   80-100a

100-120a   100-140a   100-80a   120-100b   120-100a

Fig. A.30   Results for object frog using our GH method.

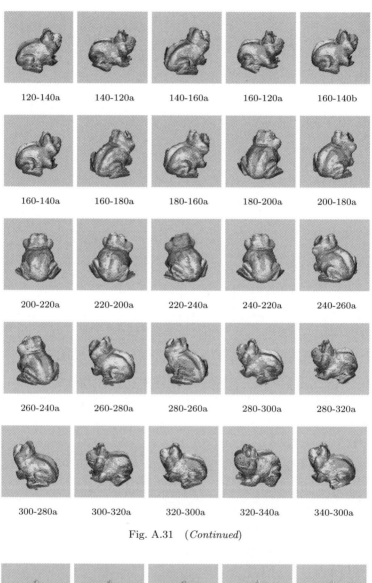

120-140a	140-120a	140-160a	160-120a	160-140b
160-140a	160-180a	180-160a	180-200a	200-180a
200-220a	220-200a	220-240a	240-220a	240-260a
260-240a	260-280a	280-260a	280-300a	280-320a
300-280a	300-320a	320-300a	320-340a	340-300a

Fig. A.31　(*Continued*)

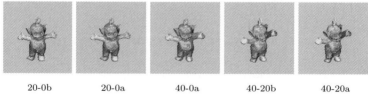

20-0b	20-0a	40-0a	40-20b	40-20a

Fig. A.32　Results for object teletubby using our GH method.

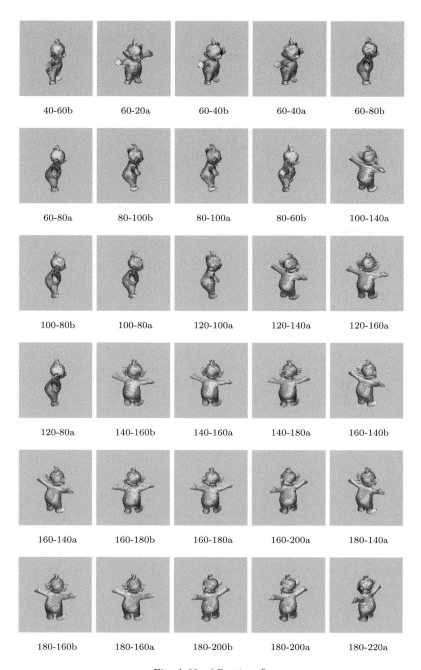

40-60b   60-20a   60-40b   60-40a   60-80b

60-80a   80-100b   80-100a   80-60b   100-140a

100-80b   100-80a   120-100a   120-140a   120-160a

120-80a   140-160b   140-160a   140-180a   160-140b

160-140a   160-180b   160-180a   160-200a   180-140a

180-160b   180-160a   180-200b   180-200a   180-220a

Fig. A.33   (*Continued*)

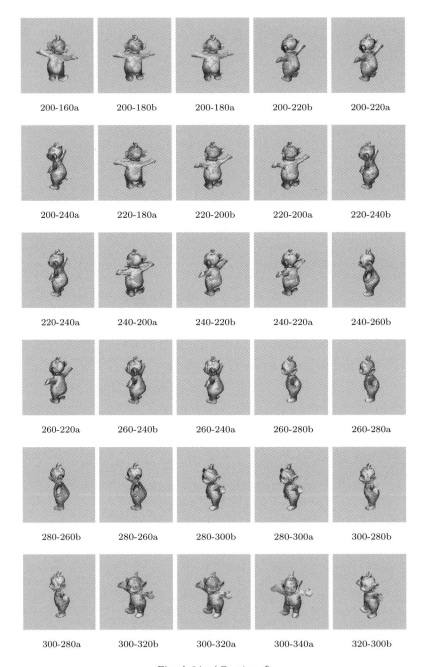

Fig. A.34   (*Continued*)

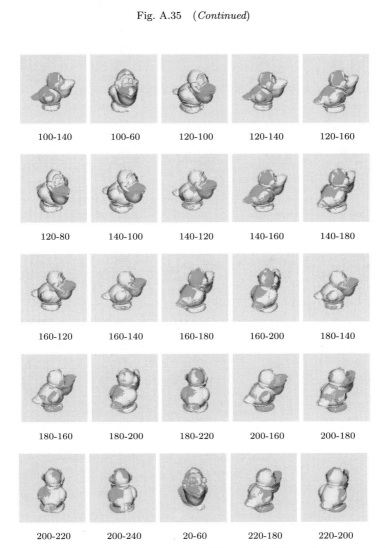

320-340b 320-340a

Fig. A.35 (*Continued*)

100-140   100-60   120-100   120-140   120-160

120-80   140-100   140-120   140-160   140-180

160-120   160-140   160-180   160-200   180-140

180-160   180-200   180-220   200-160   200-180

200-220   200-240   20-60   220-180   220-200

Fig. A.36   Results for object bird using our GH method. These view pairs are those classified as misaligned using ICP-based approaches.

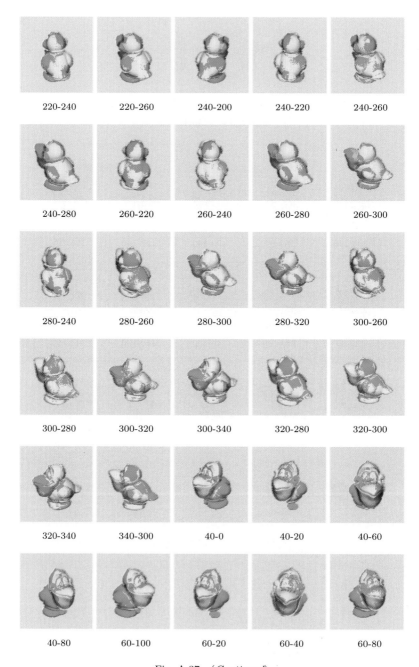

Fig. A.37   (*Continued*)

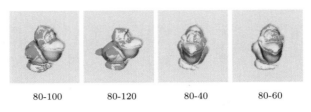

80-100   80-120   80-40   80-60

Fig. A.38   (*Continued*)

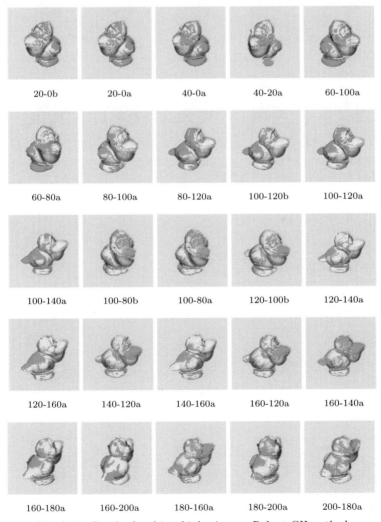

20-0b   20-0a   40-0a   40-20a   60-100a

60-80a   80-100a   80-120a   100-120b   100-120a

100-140a   100-80b   100-80a   120-100b   120-140a

120-160a   140-120a   140-160a   160-120a   160-140a

160-180a   160-200a   180-160a   180-200a   200-180a

Fig. A.39   Results for object bird using our Robust GH method.

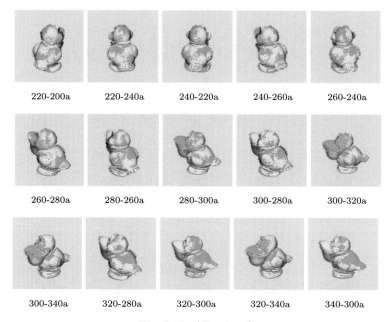

| 220-200a | 220-240a | 240-220a | 240-260a | 260-240a |

| 260-280a | 280-260a | 280-300a | 300-280a | 300-320a |

| 300-340a | 320-280a | 320-300a | 320-340a | 340-300a |

Fig. A.40   (*Continued*)

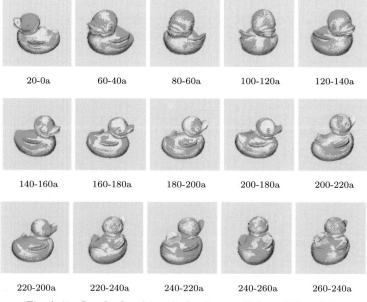

| 20-0a | 60-40a | 80-60a | 100-120a | 120-140a |

| 140-160a | 160-180a | 180-200a | 200-180a | 200-220a |

| 220-200a | 220-240a | 240-220a | 240-260a | 260-240a |

Fig. A.41   Results for object duck using our Robust GH method.

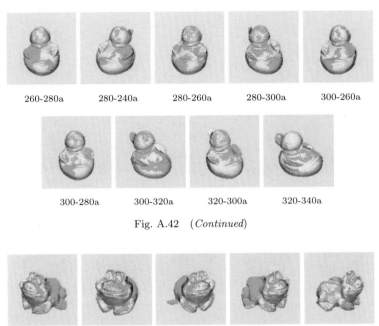

260-280a 280-240a 280-260a 280-300a 300-260a

300-280a 300-320a 320-300a 320-340a

Fig. A.42 (*Continued*)

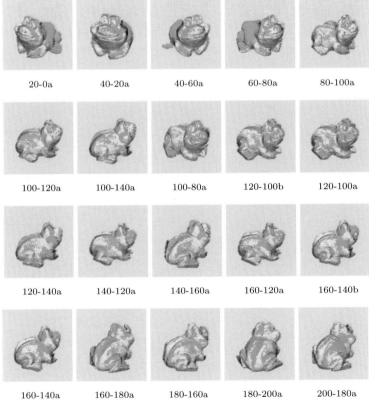

20-0a 40-20a 40-60a 60-80a 80-100a

100-120a 100-140a 100-80a 120-100b 120-100a

120-140a 140-120a 140-160a 160-120a 160-140b

160-140a 160-180a 180-160a 180-200a 200-180a

Fig. A.43 Results for object frog using our Robust GH method.

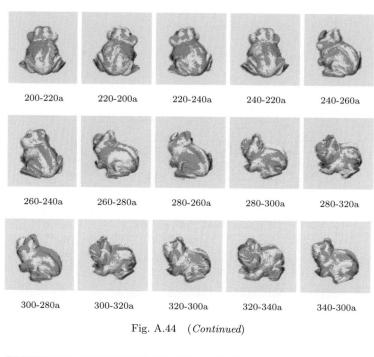

200-220a	220-200a	220-240a	240-220a	240-260a
260-240a	260-280a	280-260a	280-300a	280-320a
300-280a	300-320a	320-300a	320-340a	340-300a

Fig. A.44 (*Continued*)

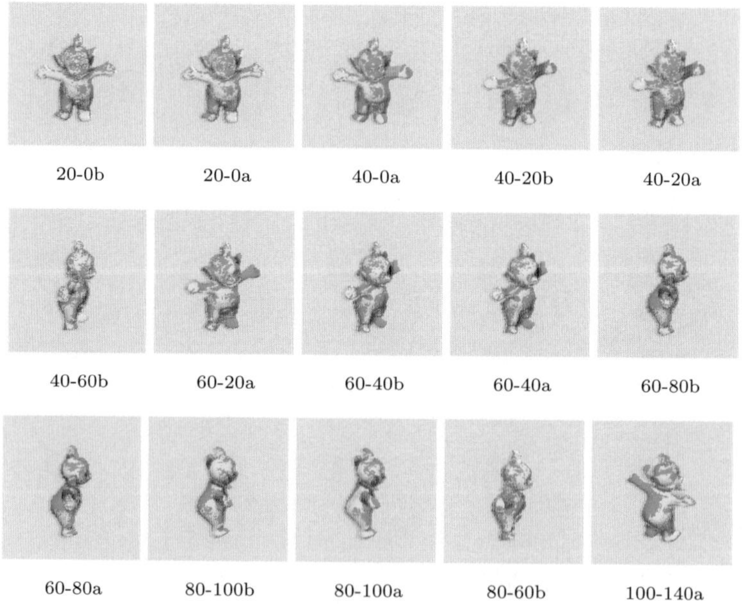

20-0b	20-0a	40-0a	40-20b	40-20a
40-60b	60-20a	60-40b	60-40a	60-80b
60-80a	80-100b	80-100a	80-60b	100-140a

Fig. A.45   Results for object teletubby using our Robust GH method.

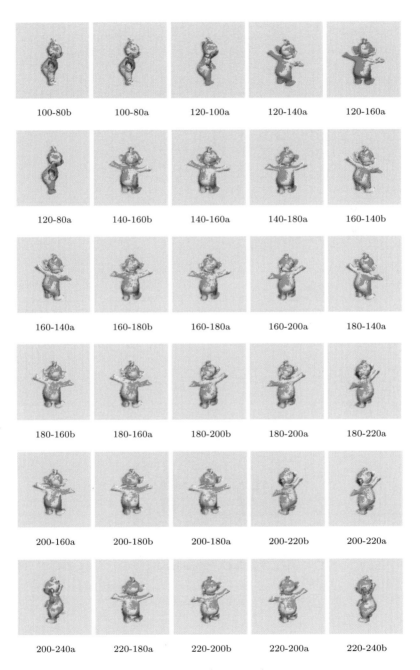

Fig. A.46 (*Continued*)

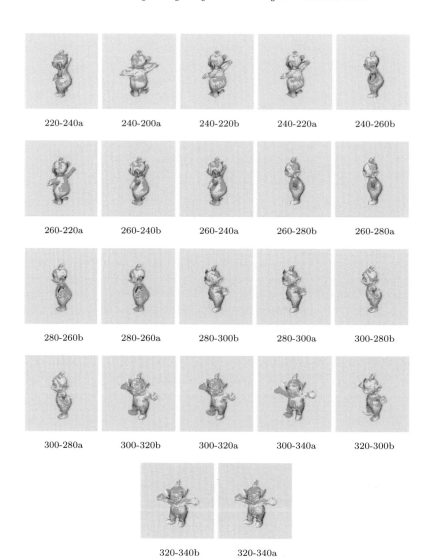

220-240a   240-200a   240-220b   240-220a   240-260b

260-220a   260-240b   260-240a   260-280b   260-280a

280-260b   280-260a   280-300b   280-300a   300-280b

300-280a   300-320b   300-320a   300-340a   320-300b

320-340b   320-340a

Fig. A.47   (*Continued*)

Bibliography

Ahmed, M., Yamany, S., Hemayed, E., Ahmed, S., Roberts, S., and Farag, A. (1997). 3D reconstruction of the human jaw from a sequence of images. *Proceedings of IEEE Conference on Computer Vision and Pattern Recognition*, pp. 646–653.

Alba, E. and Tomassini, M. (2002). Parallelism and evolutionary algorithms, *IEEE Transactions on Evolutionary Computation*, 6, 5, pp. 443–462.

Arun, K., Huang, T., and Blostein, S. (1987). Least-squares fitting of two 3-D point sets, *IEEE Transactions on Pattern Analysis and Machine Intelligence*, 9, 5, pp. 698–700.

Bellon, O. and Silva, L. (2002). New improvements to range image segmentation by edge detection, *IEEE Signal Processing Letters*, 9, 2, pp. 43–45.

Bentley, J. (1975). Multidimensional binary search trees used for associative searching, *Communications of the ACM*, 18, 9, pp. 509–517.

Bergevin, R., Soucy, M., Gagnon, H., and Laurendeau, D. (1996). Towards a general multi-view registration technique, *IEEE Transactions on Pattern Analysis and Machine Intelligence*, 18, 5, pp. 540–547.

Bernardini, F., Martin, I., Mittleman, J., Rushmeier, H., and Taubin, G. (2002). Building a digital model of michelangelo's florentine piet, *IEEE Computer Graphics & Applications*, 22, 1, pp. 59–67.

Besl, P. (1989). *Advances in Machine Vision*, chapter 1. Active Optical Range Imaging Sensors, pp. 1–63. Springer-Verlag, New York, NY.

Besl, P. and McKay, N. (1992). A method for registration of 3-D shapes, *IEEE Transactions on Pattern Analysis and Machine Intelligence*, 14, 2, pp. 239–256.

Blais, G. and Levine, M. (1995). Registering multiview range data to create 3D computer objects, *IEEE Transactions on Pattern Analysis and Machine Intelligence*, 17, 8, pp. 820–824.

Brown, L. (1992). A survey of image registration techniques, *ACM Computing Surveys*, 24, 4, pp. 325–376.

Brunnstrom, K. and Stoddart, A. (1996). Genetic algorithms for free-form surface matching. *Proceedings of the 13th International Conference on Pattern Recognition*, 4, pp. 689–693.

Chalermwat, P. and El-Ghazawi, T. (1999). Multi-resolution image registration using genetics. *Proceedings of 6th IEEE International Conference on Image Processing*, 2, pp. 452–456.

Chen, C., Hung, Y., and Cheng, J. (1999). RANSAC-based DARCES: A new approach to fast automatic registration of partially overlapping range images, *IEEE Transactions on Pattern Analysis and Machine Intelligence*, 21, 11, pp. 1229–1234.

Chen, Y. and Medioni, G. (1992). Object modeling by registration of multiple range images, *Image and Vision Computing*, 10, 3, pp. 145–155.

Chua, C. and Jarvis, R. (1996). 3D free-form surface registration and object recognition, *International Journal of Computer Vision*, 17, 1, pp. 77–99.

Cinque, L., Corzani, F., Levialdi, S., and Cucchiara, R. (2002). Improvement in range segmentation parameters tuning. *International Conference on Pattern Recognition*, 1, pp. 176–179.

Coello, C. (2000). An updated survey of GA-based multiobjective optimization techniques, *ACM Computing Surveys*, 32, 2, pp. 109–143.

Curless, B. and Levoy, M. (1996). A volumetric method for building complex models from range images. *Proceedings of the 23th Annual Conference on Computer Graphics and Interactive Techniques*, pp. 303–312.

Dalley, G. and Flynn, P. (2001). Range image registration: A software platform and empirical evaluation. *Proceedings of the 3th International Conference on 3-D Digital Imaging and Modeling*, 1, pp. 246–253.

Dalley, G. and Flynn, P. (2002). Pair-wise range image registration: A study in outlier classification, *Computer Vision and Image Understanding*, 87, 1-3, pp. 104–115.

Deb, K. (2001). *Multi-Objective Optimization Using Evolutionary Algorithms*. John Wiley & Sons.

Deb, K., Pratap, A., Agarwal, S., and Meyarivan, T. (2002). A fast and elitist multiobjective genetic algorithm: NSGA-II, *IEEE Transactions on Evolutionary Computation*, 6, 2, pp. 182–197.

Dorai, C., Wang, G., Jain, A., and Mercer, C. (1998). Registration and integration of multiple object views for 3D model construction, *IEEE Transactions on Pattern Analysis and Machine Intelligence*, 20, 1, pp. 83–89.

Eggert, D., Fitzgibbon, A., and Fisher, R. (1998). Simultaneous registration of multiple range views for use in reverse engineering of CAD models, *Computer Vision and Image Understanding*, 69, 3, pp. 253–272.

Faugeras, O. and Hebert, M. (1986). The representation, recognition, and locating of 3D objects, *International Journal of Robotics Research*, 5, 3, pp. 27–52.

Feldmar, J. and Ayache, N. (1996). Rigid, affine and locally affine registration of free-form surfaces, *International Journal of Computer Vision*, 18, 2, pp. 99–119.

Fischler, M. and Bolles, R. (1981). Random sample consensus: A paradigm for model fitting with applications to image analysis and automated cartography, *Communications of the ACM*, 24, 6, pp. 381–395.

Goldberg, D. (1989). *Genetic Algorithms in Search, Optimization and Machine Learning*. Addison-Wesley.

Gotardo, P., Bellon, O., and Silva, L. (2003a). Range image segmentation by surface extraction using an improved robust estimator. *Proceedings of IEEE Conference on Computer Vision and Pattern Recognition*, 2, pp. 33–38.

Gotardo, P., Bellon, O., Silva, L., and Boyer, K. (2003b). Range image segmentation by surface extraction using improved robust estimator and genetic algorithm, *IEEE Transactions on Systems, Man and Cybernetics, Part B*. Submitted.

Greenspan, M. and Godin, G. (2001). A nearest neighbour method for efficient ICP. *Proceedings of the 3th International Conference on 3-D Digital Imaging and Modeling*, 1, pp. 161–168.

Guibas, L. and Stolfi, J. (1985). Primitives for the manipulations of general subdivisions and the computation of Voronoi diagrams, *ACM Transactions on Graphics*, 4, 2, pp. 74–123.

Haddon, J. (1988). Generalized threshold selection for edge detection, *Pattern Recognition*, 21pp. 195–203.

Hart, W. (1994). *Adaptive Global Optimization with Local Search*. PhD thesis, University of California, San Diego.

Holland, J. (1975). *Adaptation In Natural and Artificial Systems*. The University of Michigan Press, Ann Arbour.

Horn, B. (1986). *Robot vision*. MIT Press.

Horn, B., Hilden, H., and Negahdaripour, S. (1988). Closed-form solution of absolute orientation using orthonormal matrices, *Journal of the Optical Society of America - A*, 5, 7, pp. 1127–1135.

Huber, D. and Hebert, M. (2003). 3D modeling using a statistical sensor model and stochastic search. *Proceedings of the IEEE Conference on Computer Vision and Pattern Recognition*, pp. 858–865.

Ikeuchi, K. and Sato, Y., editors (2001). *Modeling From Reality*. Kluwer Academic Publishers.

Ingber, L. (1989). Very fast simulated re-annealing, *Mathematical Computer Modelling*, 12pp. 967–973.

Johnson, A. and Hebert, M. (1999). Using spin images for efficient object recognition in cluttered 3D scenes, *IEEE Transactions on Pattern Analysis and Machine Intelligence*, 21, 5, pp. 433–449.

Khare, V., Yao, X., and Deb, K. (2003). Performance scaling of multi-objective evolutionary algorithms. *Second International Conference on Evolutionary Multi-Criterion Optimization*, 2632 of *Lecture Notes in Computer Science*, pp. 376–390.

Kirkpatrick, S., Gelatt, C., and Vecchi, M. (1983). Optimization by simulated annealing, *Science*, 220, 4598, pp. 671–680.

Leitao, H. and Stolfi, J. (2002). A multiscale method for the reassembly of two-dimensional fragmented objects, *IEEE Transactions on Pattern Analysis and Machine Intelligence*, 24, 9, pp. 1239–1251.

Levoy, M., Pulli, K., Curless, B., Rusinkiewicz, S., Koller, D., Pereira, L., Ginzton, M., Anderson, S., Davis, J., Ginsberg, J., Shade, J., and Fulk, D. (2000). The digital michelangelo project: 3D scanning of large statues. *Proceedings of the 27th Annual Conference on Computer Graphics and In-*

teractive Techniques, pp. 131–144.

Liu, Y. and Rodrigues, M. (2002). Geometrical analysis of two sets of 3D correspondence data patterns for the registration of free-form shapes, *Journal of Intelligent and Robotic Systems*, 33, 4, pp. 409–436.

Lohn, J., Kraus, W., and Haith, G. (2002). Comparing a coevolutionary genetic algorithm for multiobjective optimization. *Proceedings of the 2002 IEEE Congress on Evolutionary Computation*, pp. 1157–1162.

Lucchese, L., Doretto, G., and Cortelazzo, G. (2002). A frequency domain technique for range data registration, *IEEE Transactions on Pattern Analysis and Machine Intelligence*, 24, 11, pp. 1468–1484.

Man, K., Tang, K., and Kwong, S. (1996). Genetic algorithms: concepts and applications, *IEEE Transactions on Industrial Eletronics*, 43, 5, pp. 519–534.

Masuda, T. (2002). Registration and integration of multiple range images by matching signed distance fields for object shape modeling, *Computer Vision and Image Understanding*, 87, 1-3, pp. 51–65.

Masuda, T. and Yokoya, N. (1995). A robust method for registration and segmentation of multiple range images, *Computer Vision and Image Understanding*, 61, 3, pp. 295–307.

Pratt, V. (1987). Direct least-squares fitting of algebraic surfaces, *Computer Graphics*, 21, 4, pp. 145–152.

Reed, M. and Allen, P. (1999). 3D modeling from range imagery: An incremental method with a planning component, *Image and Vision Computing*, 17, 2, pp. 99–111.

Renders, J. and Flasse, S. (1996). Hybrid methods using genetic algorithms for global optimization, *IEEE Transactions on Systems, Man and Cybernetics, Part B*, 26, 2, pp. 243–258.

Robertson, C. and Fisher, R. (2002). Parallel evolutionary registration of range data, *Computer Vision and Image Understanding*, 87, 1-3, pp. 39–50.

Rodrigues, M., Fisher, R., and Liu, Y. (2002). Special issue on registration and fusion of range images, *Computer Vision and Image Understanding*, 87, 1-3, pp. 1–7.

Rusinkiewicz, S. and Levoy, M. (2001a). Efficient variants of the ICP algorithm. *Proceedings of the 3th International Conference on 3-D Digital Imaging and Modeling*, 1, pp. 145–152.

Rusinkiewicz, S. and Levoy, M. (2001b). Streaming QSplat: a viewer for networked visualization of large, dense models. *Symposium on Interactive 3D Graphics*, pp. 63–68.

Sahoo, P., Soltani, S., Wong, A., and Chen, Y. (1988). A survey of thresholding techniques, *CVGIP - Graphical Models and Image Processing*, 41, 2, pp. 233–260.

Sappa, A., Restrepo-Specht, A., and Devy, M. (2001). Range image registration by using an edge-based representation. *International Symposium on Intelligent Robotic Systems*, pp. 167–176.

Sawai, H. and Adachi, S. (1999). Parallel distributed processing of a parameter-free GA by using hierarchical migration methods. *Proceedings of the Genetic and Evolutionary Computation Conference*, 1, pp. 579–586.

Schutz, C., Jost, T., and Hugli, H. (1998). Multi-feature matching algorithm for free-form 3D surface recognition. *Proceedings 14th International Conference on Pattern Recognition*, pp. 982–984.

Sharp, G., Lee, S., and Wehe, D. (2002). ICP registration using invariant features, *IEEE Transactions on Pattern Analysis and Machine Intelligence*, 24, 1, pp. 90–102.

Shum, H., Hebert, M., Ikeuchi, K., and Reddy, R. (1997). An integral approach to free-form object modeling, *IEEE Transactions on Pattern Analysis and Machine Intelligence*, 19, 12, pp. 1366–1370.

Silva, L., Bellon, O., and Boyer, K. (2003a). Enhanced, robust genetic algorithms for multiview range image registration. *Proceedings of the 4th International Conference on 3-D Digital Imaging and Modeling*.

Silva, L., Bellon, O., and Boyer, K. (2003b). Robust multiview range image registration. *Proceedings of the 16th Brazilian Symposium on Computer Graphics and Image Processing*.

Silva, L., Bellon, O., and Boyer, K. (2003c). Robust range image registration using the surface interpenetration measure and enhanced genetic algorithms, *IEEE Transactions on Pattern Analysis and Machine Intelligence*. Submitted.

Silva, L., Bellon, O., Boyer, K., and Gotardo, P. (2003d). Low-overlap range image registration for archaeological applications. *Proceedings of IEEE/CVPR Workshop on Applications of Computer Vision in Archaeology*.

Silva, L., Bellon, O., and Gotardo, P. (2001). Edge-based image segmentation using curvature sign maps from reflectance and range images. *Proceedings of 8th IEEE International Conference on Image Processing*, 1, pp. 730–734.

Silva, L., Bellon, O., and Gotardo, P. (2002). A global-to-local approach for robust range image segmentation. *Proceedings of 9th IEEE International Conference on Image Processing*, 1, pp. 773–776.

Silva, L., Bellon, O., Gotardo, P., and Boyer, K. (2003e). Range image registration using enhanced genetic algorithms. *Proceedings of 10th IEEE International Conference on Image Processing*, 2, pp. 711–714.

Sinha, T., Cash, D., Weil, R., Galloway, R., and Miga, M. (2003). Laser range scanning for cortical surface characterization during neurosurgery. *Proceedings of SPIE Medical Imaging*, 5029, pp. 98–107.

Stein, F. and Medioni, G. (1992). Structural indexing: Efficient 3-D object recognition, *IEEE Transactions on Pattern Analysis and Machine Intelligence*, 14, 2, pp. 125–145.

Stoddart, A. and Hilton, A. (1996). Registration of multiple point sets. *Proceedings IEEE International Conference on Pattern Recognition*, pp. 40–44.

Torr, P. and Zisserman, A. (2000). MLESAC: A new robust estimator with application to estimating image geometry, *Computer Vision and Image Understanding*, 78, 1, pp. 138–156.

Turk, G. and Levoy, M. (1994). Zippered polygon meshes from range images. *Proceedings of the 21st Annual Conference on Computer Graphics*, pp. 311–318.

Vieira, E., Bellon, O., and Silva, L. (2002). Minerao de imagens, *Revista de Informatica Terica e Aplicada*, 9, 2, pp. 67–96.

Wyngaerd, J. and Gool, L. (2002). Automatic crude patch registration: Toward automatic 3D model building, *Computer Vision and Image Understanding*, 87, 1-3, pp. 8–26.

Yamany, S. and Farag, A. (1999). Free-form surface registration using surface signatures. *Proceedings of International Conference on Computer Vision*, pp. 1098–1104.

Youssef, H., Sait, S., and Adiche, H. (2001). Evolutionary algorithms, simulated annealing and tabu search: a comparative study, *Engineering Applications of Artificial Intelligence*, 14pp. 167–181.

Zhang, Z. (1994). Iterative point matching for registration of free-form curves and surfaces, *International Journal of Computer Vision*, 13, 2, pp. 119–152.

Zitzler, E., Laumanns, M., and Thiele, L. (2002). SPEA2: Improving the strength pareto evolutionary algorithm for multiobjective optimization. Giannakoglou, K., Tsahalis, D., Periaux, J., Papaliliou, K., and Fogarty, T., editors, *Evolutionary Methods for Design, Optimisation and Control with Application to Industrial Problems. Proceedings of the EUROGEN2001 Conference*, pp. 95–100.

Index